# ADVANCE PRAISE

"In *Fire Doesn't Innovate*, Kip Boyle helps busy executives understand their cyber risks and, more importantly, take the critical steps necessary to remediate them. The book provides an easy-to-follow guide to solve a highly complex problem."

—MARC GOODMAN, AUTHOR, *FUTURE CRIMES*

"The best technical tools can only do so much to protect your company. If you don't have the accompanying education and training—that human element—you are going to lose the fight for cybersecurity. Kip provides that human element."

—SANDRA KURACK, CEO, SCHOOL EMPLOYEES CREDIT UNION OF WASHINGTON

"Kip brings his years of experience of 'being in the trenches' to teach the reader that cybersecurity is a business problem, not a technical problem. He uses real-world examples of risks, how to mitigate them, and how to identify future threats."

—KYLE WELSH, CISO, BOEING EMPLOYEES CREDIT UNION

*"Kip puts leaders in a position to drive the conversation around cybersecurity in their company."*

—GARRETT WHITNEY, CIO, DELTA
DENTAL OF WASHINGTON

*"Kip gives the reader the tools they need to better understand risks as they come, assessing their options and doing the right thing while protecting themselves and their companies. Now they can greatly reduce their reliance on vendors and the media as sources for what's truly important about their cybersecurity."*

—ANDREAS BRAENDLE, CIO, MILLIMAN

*"This book is full of compelling stories that make cybersecurity very accessible to the nontechnical reader."*

—RAJ SAMANI, MCAFEE FELLOW, CHIEF SCIENTIST

*"Cyberthreats continue to evolve. They probe our firm's IT infrastructure, and more importantly, they attempt to deceive our staff. Fire Doesn't Innovate can help your firm recognize the threats, develop effective ways to manage a cybersecurity program, and build a culture of caution and awareness."*

—LEE MARSH, CEO, BERGERABAM

*"Fire Doesn't Innovate is a tremendous summation of the many lessons learned by a seasoned cybersecurity leader over decades of work from the technical trenches to the boardroom.*

*This book will coach you to win in cybersecurity—for your customers, your employees, and your shareholders."*

—JOEL SCAMBRAY, AUTHOR, *HACKING EXPOSED*, VICE
PRESIDENT OF SOFTWARE SECURITY, NCC GROUP

"*Kip provides readers with an important recognition of cybersecurity risks and a pragmatic, ongoing approach to addressing those risks."*

—GORDON S. TANNURA, SENIOR VICE PRESIDENT, VISA

*"As an attorney advising clients on cybersecurity, I'll be advising my clients to read this book to help guide them on their journey to reasonable cybersecurity!"*

—JAKE BERNSTEIN, CYBERSECURITY
PRACTICE LEADER, NEWMAN DU WORS

"*True cybersecurity is not about the latest gadgets or products, but rather a holistic blend of education, policies, and tools that addresses one of the most complex issues of our day. As Fire Doesn't Innovate shows, Kip has both the attention to detail and business communication skills to advise the reader in developing a viable approach to managing changing cyber risks."*

—STEPHEN WHITLOCK, CHIEF CYBERSECURITY
STRATEGIST, COMMERCIAL AVIATION
SERVICES, THE BOEING COMPANY

*"Executive leaders commonly either underestimate the importance of cybersecurity or don't understand the complex nature of ever-evolving cyber risks. Kip's book is full of compelling stories that bring cybersecurity home for the nontechnical reader."*

—RALPH JOHNSON, CISO, LOS ANGELES
COUNTY, CALIFORNIA

*"With Kip's book, readers can now greatly reduce their reliance on vendors and the media as sources for what's truly important about their cybersecurity."*

—ANDREW WHITAKER, CISO, CITY OF SEATTLE

*"Kip's book is full of stories that not only bring awareness and urgency to the cybersecurity conversation but also provide a path forward for the nontechnical leader."*

—TOM TAYLOR, CHIEF RISK OFFICER,
MUTUAL OF ENUMCLAW INSURANCE

*"Cybersecurity is not my area of expertise. Fortunately for me and for our organization, Fire Doesn't Innovate walked us through a systematic process to be both effective and efficient in protecting against cyber risks."*

—JOEL GENDELMAN, CEO, N2UITIVE

*"This book is the culmination of more than twenty-five years of Kip's hands-on experience balancing people, processes, and technology to reduce company-wide cybersecurity risks."*

—MICHAEL RIEMER, SERIAL ENTREPRENEUR
AND COFOUNDER OF THE FIRST
COMMERCIAL ANTIVIRUS COMPANY

"A must-read for the C-suite and security professionals."

"I'm giving a copy to each of my executives and everyone on my team—it's that helpful!"

"Kip's book gives practical, understandable direction for constructing a continually improving cybersecurity program."

"Even with the high level of publicity that cyberattacks receive these days, executive leaders continue to underestimate the complex nature of cyber risk, often defining it as a technology problem best handled by the IT department. Kip widens the reader's aperture by showing that managing cybersecurity is a business risk like any other, one that needs executive involvement to be successful."

"Many organizations are unable to achieve a basic level of cybersecurity hygiene, much less analyze and prioritize their cybersecurity risks. Kip's book gives the reader a framework to do both."

*"Anyone who implements the practical measures in this book will enhance their overall risk management as a result."*

*"I met Kip ten years ago and recognized his leadership in seeing cybersecurity as a people problem, a business challenge, and an opportunity. It's great to see Kip's experience now accessible to the next generation of cybersecurity leaders."*

*"As both a speaker and an author, Kip focuses on present-day threats to our business and provides solutions to mitigate current cyberthreats."*

# FIRE DOESN'T INNOVATE

# FIRE
# DOESN'T
# INNOVATE

THE EXECUTIVE'S PRACTICAL GUIDE TO THRIVING

IN THE FACE OF EVOLVING CYBER RISKS

## KIP BOYLE

LIONCREST

PUBLISHING

FIRE DOESN'T INNOVATE

*The Executive's Practical Guide to Thriving*
*in the Face of Evolving Cyber Risks*

ISBN   978-1-5445-1319-5 *Paperback*

978-1-5445-1318-8 *Ebook*

*For executives everywhere who want to make their organizations, and our economy, more resilient by managing cyber as a business risk. Thank you.*

# CONTENTS

INTRODUCTION............................................................15

**PART ONE: THE BASICS OF CYBERSECURITY**

1. FIRE DOESN'T INNOVATE...BUT CYBERCRIMINALS DO.......31
2. CYBER RISK MANAGEMENT ............................................55
3. GERM THEORY AND CYBERHYGIENE ..............................87
4. CYBERHYGIENE AND WORK TRAVEL............................125

**PART TWO: YOUR CYBER RISK MANAGEMENT GAME PLAN**

5. PHASE 1 ...................................................................149
6. PHASE 2 ...................................................................195
7. PHASE 3 ...................................................................235

CONCLUSION............................................................251
APPENDIX ................................................................255
ACKNOWLEDGMENTS ................................................259
ABOUT THE AUTHOR ................................................263

# INTRODUCTION

## CYBERSECURITY IS A BUSINESS PROBLEM, NOT A TECHNICAL PROBLEM

A single email could cost you $56 million.

At least that's what happened with Austria-based aerospace company FACC, a midmarket business that supplies spare parts to Boeing and Airbus. In late 2015, a clever cybercriminal successfully manipulated someone inside FACC's finance department to move $56 million into the criminal's account. The offender pulled off this phishing attack, which is a socially engineered attempt to steal your money or your company's money, by sneaking onto the CEO's email and imitating the quirks of his writing style to craft a perfectly believable email to a finance department worker.

Months later, in January 2016, the company disclosed the theft publicly: FACC was able to recover about $11 million of their losses, but due in large part to this incident, the company reported a $22 million total loss for 2015.

Their official statement about the incident, and the dismissal of the CEO, looked like this:

> The supervisory board came to the conclusion that Mr. Walter Stephan has severely violated his duties, in particular, in relation to the "fake president" incident, and Mr. Robert Machtlinger was appointed as interim CEO of FACC.

Their stock price fell 17 percent when they made the announcement. It wasn't just the CEO who took the fall either. FACC also fired the CFO and the person in the finance department who fell for the business email compromise, which used to be known as a "fake president" scam.

### WHAT IS A FAKE PRESIDENT?

A "fake president" email scam is an old term for cyber-attacks like the one FACC fell victim to. Now they're referred to as "business email compromises," meaning a person outside the organization pretends to be the president (or CEO, or CTO, or any executive) in order to fraudulently receive money from the company.

More than a year after the FACC incident, in May 2017, the FBI issued a notice that these business email compromise scams have cost businesses approximately $5 billion worldwide over the previous three years, and the frequency is only rising. From October 2013 to May 2018, 78,617 incidents were reported, with total losses topping $12.5 billion. In the United State alone, 41,058 companies were hit for $2.93 billion worth of losses.

## REAL EXAMPLES OF BUSINESS
## EMAIL COMPROMISES

To: Accounts Payable

From: Jay@company.com

Subject: RE: Business Consulting Services

Hi Marie,

Are you at the office?

Can we send a wire out today? Kindly find out from the bank the cutoff time for international payments also.

I'll be busy, email me.

Regards,

Jay

The targeted employee initially responded, asking if "Jay" had the information to make the payment, and stating that the cutoff time for international payments was 2:30 p.m. Luckily, the employee reported the email fraud attempt, so the bad guys didn't get their payday— this time.

This is a great example why cybersecurity awareness training is so important! Your employees are many times your first, or only, line of defense.

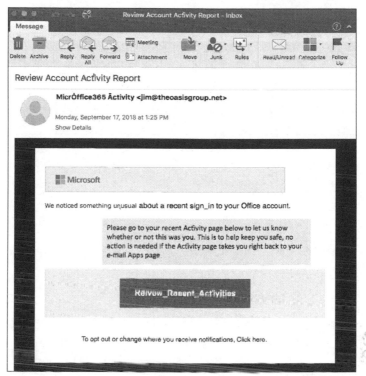

Here's another example of a business email compromise. Notice the suspicious markings in the subject line as well as in the body of the message.

The messages in a business email compromise scam will look legitimate because the cybercriminal has been able to either hack into the company's email server and copy the executive's style of writing or, if the criminal can't get into the server, they can technically mask the source of the email so that it doesn't arouse suspicion.

However, despite the technological aspects of a business email compromise scam, it's not actually taking advantage of your company's technology. In fact, it perfectly exemplifies the most counterintuitive aspect of cyber-security: it's an attack on people's *emotions*.

## HOW TO MAINTAIN YOUR REPUTATION IN A DIGITALLY DANGEROUS WORLD

You probably know that cybersecurity is something you should focus on in your company. Maybe you've been putting off dealing with it because there are more important aspects of your business that need your attention. And let's face it, even if you identify as a tech expert, your next step is not obvious.

Look at the FACC example. That breach had nothing to do with technology being exploited. Sure, the cyber-criminal used technology to send the email, but none of the company's technological defenses or controls were compromised.

It was an attack on a person—and a process, not technology. More specifically, it was an attack on the *lack of process*. FACC didn't have enough reasonable cyber-security measures in place to help manage the risk that the cybercriminal posed, such as a training program or a dual-authorization process to move large amounts of cash.

As an executive, your bread and butter should be having

great people who are trained appropriately and have great processes in critical areas of your business, such as sales, order fulfillment, and accounts receivable. Why would you approach cybersecurity any differently?

Just like every other aspect of your job as an executive, you'll find cybersecurity success by working through other people. Although there is no such thing as a perfect prevention plan, you can enhance your reputation as a company of integrity, one that implements effective practices to protect your stakeholders by safeguarding your organization's assets, including your customers' data.

As a result, when your competitors inevitably fail to stop cyberthreats and can't keep their doors open, you will be standing strong when the dust settles, with your reputation and data intact. You'll see greater revenues, larger customers, and feel a greater sense of control over your company.

**UNEXPECTED CONSEQUENCES OF STOLEN DATA**

Having a single department compromised could change the trajectory of your company forever. Look at payroll data, for example. If someone got access to that information, they would have your employees' full names, addresses, phone numbers, social security numbers, places of business, and annual salaries. That's more than enough information to open credit accounts and borrow money in their name, which your employee would never get back. In other words, that's enough to destroy individual people's reputations and lives, not just your company's bottom line.

## REASONABLE (IF IMPERFECT) CYBERSECURITY

In this book, you'll learn how to handle cybersecurity like any other business risk: as something you can manage without being a subject matter expert. You'll learn how to utilize the personnel and technological resources you already have at your disposal to properly deal with cyber risks. You likely have more skills that translate to cybersecurity than you realize. I'll help you unlock those skills.

In part 1 of the book, you'll learn the common patterns for cybercrimes, how to utilize what I call good cyberhygiene to prevent them, and how to encourage your team to protect the organizational assets, and their own personal assets as well.

Part 2 is dedicated to helping you develop your own Cyber

Risk Management Game Plan, which is a specially modified version of the same service we give our customers, including specific questionnaires, scoring sheets, and reports to help you identify, prioritize, and protect against your company's unique cybersecurity threats. (We've also created an online tool, the Cyber Risk Workbook, to automate your work. More on that in part 2.)

## THE INTERNET: BUILT FOR ACADEMIA AND THE MILITARY, NOT COMMERCE

The Internet was never designed to be a secure place of commerce; it was designed to be a network of freely shared data between colleges and military institutions. In 1992, when I first started working in cybersecurity as an Air Force officer, the average citizen did not have access to the Internet. Even if they did have access, they would have had nothing to use it for. At that time, commercial activities on the Internet were prohibited.

The early Internet had one primary goal: to provide reliable communication between academic and military entities, even if random parts of the network went offline. Confidentiality was not a goal of the Internet because the research-heavy culture of academia prioritized the free, quick, and easy sharing of information, as did the research and development organizations within the military.

> The Internet was not built for commerce, yet that's what we use it for every day of our lives.

Ironically, as an Air Force officer in the early 1990s, my most important job was to ensure the data security of the F-22 "Raptor" during the final stages of its initial production at dozens of locations across the United States. The "Raptor" was so sophisticated that it was essentially a flying computer, calculating thousands of microcorrections per second just to get off the ground and stay in the air. Our enemies would have loved to get their hands on the data of these high-performance jet fighters. Therefore, although it was rare for the time, I was tasked with actually *securing* data rather than making it freely available, like most institutions with access to the Internet.

To achieve my F-22 mission, I worked directly with the US Air Force and individual defense contractors such as Lockheed Martin, Boeing, Pratt & Whitney, and their subcontractors in Ohio, Georgia, Washington, Arizona, Florida, Colorado, and Edwards Air Force Base in California.

As I left the military in 1997, online commerce was blossoming. The policies that restricted commerce on the Internet were about to be repealed, and companies like Amazon.com were about to actually sell goods over the Internet for the first time.

It was nothing short of a revolution.

I next went to work at Stanford Research Institute in Menlo Park, California, where I helped innovative organizations use the Internet to grow their businesses securely.

During that time, I helped clients such as the Federal Reserve Bank of the United States figure out secure payment processing platforms to move hundreds of millions of dollars among banks around the world. I also helped private companies such as NTT Data in Japan, Mitsubishi, DuPont, and Merck solve cybersecurity problems years before the rest of the market even knew what cybersecurity was.

In 2003, I accepted a fantastic role as chief information security officer (CISO) at what was then known as PEMCO Financial Services in Seattle. While at PEMCO, I learned how to manage cybersecurity for a host of highly regulated businesses: a personal lines property and casualty insurance company, a credit card and debit card transaction processor, a community bank, a large credit union, and a technology services provider that delivered managed desktop computers, servers, and networks to them all.

Eventually, in June 2015, I launched my own company, Cyber Risk Opportunities. Our mission is to help executives like you thrive as cyber risk managers. I launched the company to answer the following question: Given my uniquely intimate knowledge of cybersecurity and all that I'm capable of doing, what is the most impactful way I can help the most people?

Founding my own company was the best answer to that question. But that's also why I'm writing this book: so I can help you learn how to make smart cyber risk-related decisions, which will make your organization safer and more reliable, given the increasingly dangerous Internet.

To that end, this book is not going to teach you a specific step-by-step guide on how to accomplish the right technological configuration for your computer to achieve perfect cybersecurity. Perfect cybersecurity is impossible, and that shouldn't be your goal anyway.

This book is a practical cybersecurity toolkit for you, the busy executive, not an in-depth technical analysis of cybersecurity.

## YOUR NEVER-ENDING ARMS RACE

You weren't born knowing how to read financial statements or how to manage people. You had to learn those skills, and you had to learn them from another person—whether face-to-face or from a book or video. However, you found someone who was very good at what you wanted to accomplish, and you learned as much as possible from them.

Likewise, unless you're the CFO, you don't have to know *every* facet of financial statements, or know how to manage every single expert in your company. Similarly, you don't need intimate knowledge about every nuance in cybersecurity. You just need a mentor who does.

As you read through this book, think of me as your mentor: I'm going to teach you what you *need* to know—and no more—in order to practice reasonable cybersecurity for you and your organization.

Here's your first lesson: cyber is a new kind of threat—one that is very different from traditional threats, such as fire. Consider reading this book and embracing its principles as guarding against a devastating fire. Now that humans have more than one hundred years of fire prevention experience in big cities and suburbs, you know a fire is unlikely to affect you, but on the off chance that it does, you want to be protected. But fire doesn't innovate. The chemical reactions that make up a fire and the unique damage it causes will be the same forever. Because of that, the combination of modern building codes, materials, and insurance have removed most of the burden from our shoulders.

Cyber risks, on the other hand, are constantly evolving. As soon as we figure out a reliable combination of preventive, detective, and corrective controls, the cybercriminals figure out new ways to strike. It's a never-ending arms race. Are you ready to learn how to evolve with them?

# PART ONE

# THE BASICS OF CYBERSECURITY

Maybe you've tried to learn cybersecurity before, but you were put off because nobody explained it in a way you could understand. I assure you that this book is not full of technical jargon. This book is written for you, the busy executive. Part 1 of this book will explain the basics of cybersecurity in accessible terms. Part 2 will provide you with a step-by-step method of creating a cyber risk management game plan for your company. We even created an online Cyber Risk Workbook to help automate your work.

Drawing on common metaphors, simple examples, case studies, and knowledge you already have as a business leader, I will help you internalize the basics of cybersecurity in a way that is nested in concepts you already understand.

# FIRE DOESN'T INNOVATE...BUT CYBERCRIMINALS DO

Since we first discovered fire, it has been both a tool and a menace for human beings.

In the late 1800s, Chicago and Seattle both burned to the ground. Those cities grew so fast that they didn't fully mitigate the inherent risks of their growth. The fire-resistant materials and regulations couldn't keep up. All of those people needed fire to heat their homes and run their businesses, but they didn't know how to use it safely at scale.

After those cities burned to the ground, they didn't outlaw

fire. How could they? They had to figure out ways to *control* it. They discovered that fire was actually comprised of three ingredients: heat, oxygen, and fuel. If they could deprive it of a single ingredient, they could extinguish the fire or prevent it from starting.

Over time, they figured out how to regulate fire prevention and control. They did research and discovered which materials were fire resistant. They rebuilt their cities from brick and mortar, rather than wood, and created indoor sprinkler systems. They passed laws requiring firewalls between apartments, better-funded fire departments, and fire hydrants close to homes. Thus, we learned how to use fire in a scalable way that made it useful and low risk. And on the chance that we couldn't control the fire, we created fire insurance. Because we had learned the finite number of ways fire spread and how to stop it, we could definitively prove we'd taken preventive measures and pay less money in fire insurance premiums. In large part, that's how we transformed fire from a menace to a tool.

We are going through the same evolution with the Internet and our digital assets. We need computers the same way we need fire to cook food and heat buildings. The only problem, believe it or not, is that we haven't lost any major cities or corporations to cyberattacks...yet. And that's one reason why we haven't figured out a definitive list of best practices to bring the menace of cyberattacks under control once and for all.

But the other, bigger reason is that fire doesn't innovate. Once you build a house out of bricks, a fire isn't going to figure out how to burn brick and mortar. Cybercriminals and cybersoldiers—and by extension cyber risks—constantly evolve. There will never be a definitive list of measures you can take to prevent all cyberattacks. The best you can do is learn how cyber risk has evolved, where it's going, and the actions you and your business *can* take to manage your risks, even if you can't eliminate them completely. And then repeat this cycle every year. Forever.

## THE DARK WEB

People stealing assets is a problem as old as possession itself. Up until very recently, if someone wanted to steal something from you, they had to physically take it from you. In business, theft meant someone stole boxes off your company's delivery truck while the driver was distracted, or an insider embezzled money by altering financial records, or a cashier simply stuffed company cash in their pocket while no one was looking. But times have changed. Criminals don't need access to your delivery trucks or physical cash to steal from you anymore. They can now take your assets over the Internet.

The unique characteristics of digital assets have completely changed the nature of possession and theft as we know it. Imagine someone breaks into your building and steals a physical file out of your office, which is full of bank statements and other sensitive information. Assuming you don't have any copies on hand, you've now lost that information. However, if someone steals a *digital* copy of your sensitive data, you still have your data, but someone else does too.

What that means is that rather than being stolen once, your data can be stolen many times. Once someone steals a copy of your data, that copy can be copied repeatedly with all of the fidelity of the original. Instead of being a photocopy of a photocopy of a photocopy—which becomes blurry and difficult to read—a copied digital asset is an exact duplicate.

This is a completely new paradigm of theft. Instead of being stolen once, your assets can be stolen and traded an infinite number of times.

This trading of sensitive information most often occurs on the Dark Web, as it's called.

## WHAT IS THE DARK WEB?

For those unfamiliar, the Dark Web is the portion of the Internet that is unreachable through conventional means such as a search engine or common hyperlinks. You have to take deliberate actions to get to it. Imagine a dark alley where illicit goods and services are traded out of sight of government authorities. That's the physical version of the Dark Web, except unlike the dark alley, the Dark Web is scaled globally. It is one massive back alley with millions of participants.

To access the Dark Web, a person must not only manually enter a specific web address, but they also have to use a special piece of technology. The same way you use a browser, such as Google Chrome or Firefox, to access the Internet, people use a special browser to access the Dark Web. The TOR Browser uses the TOR network, which is short for The Onion Router network. Interestingly, TOR was originally a creation of the US government, the same people who brought us the Internet. They made TOR as a means to place confidential information on the Internet while still making it restricted to the public.

However innocuous its original intentions, TOR protocol has been hijacked for more sinister purposes. Anyone can access the TOR network, meaning anyone can access the back alley of the Internet: the Dark Web.

People sell everything on the Dark Web, from stolen credit card information and company payroll information to weapons, drugs, gambling, and personal services of all kinds—including sexual services and murders for hire.

It's easy to read this information and feel scared of this vast and dangerous world that you likely never knew existed. I want to stress that I'm presenting facts so that you can be informed and learn how to protect your data. Digital risks have evolved to include trading information and digital and physical assets across a global network of cybercriminals.

There's no reason to fear if you know what you're up against and you learn how to deal with it as constructively as possible.

## CYBER RISK IS JUST ANOTHER BUSINESS RISK

Cyber risk, by definition, is the chance that your digital assets will be compromised in a way that will hurt your reputation, your bank account, your ability to conduct business, and travel when and where you want.

Every executive manages risks: sales, order fulfillments, accounts receivable. Cyber risk is simply another item on that list.

Your company will go bankrupt if you don't sell any products. That's obvious. It will also go out of business if you sell products but can't deliver them. You still won't survive if your company sells products, delivers them, but doesn't collect money for them. Seems obvious, right? If you don't manage risks in all of those parts of the process, you will lose your company.

Here's the less obvious aspect of your business risks: unaccounted cyber risks can cause you to go bankrupt in exactly the same ways. Not only that, but the cybercriminals threatening your business are constantly evolving. They are complex organizations just like your company.

Cybercriminal organizations (and the foreign intelligence services that protect and benefit from them) are just another competitor for your company. Treat them as anything less and you're missing your best shot at dealing with them effectively.

## CYBERCRIMINALS: AN EVOLUTION FROM INDIVIDUALS TO INTERNATIONAL ORGANIZATIONS

It hasn't always been this way. In the past, the people who caused trouble on the Internet weren't out for money. They were individuals whose goal was to have fun, or groups with political agendas. That was the old Internet. On the new Internet, all of those players are still in the game, but they've been eclipsed by groups of organized criminals.

The Tony Sopranos and Tony Montanas of the world aren't only in the streets anymore. They're online, and they can evolve faster than ever.

## BOGACHEV: THE MODERN CYBERCRIMINAL

The Internet hasn't only attracted organized criminals and armies. It's allowed them to work together. The poster child for this phenomenon is a Russian cybercriminal named Bogachev. He is on the FBI's most wanted list, where he's listed with a $3 million reward for his capture.

What makes Bogachev so notorious? He's produced the most prolific results on account of his malicious digital techniques, and he lives openly in a mansion on the Black Sea. Born in 1983, he represents a completely new class of criminal: he's the millennial mobster. Over the course of seven years, using digital weapons, he's been able to steal more than $100 million from Western banks.

He was able to steal all of this money in part because he had the Russian Foreign Intelligence Service protecting him and his activities, and probably providing him with digital weapons, because he provided them with access to information they wanted.

## WHAT ARE DIGITAL WEAPONS?

In order to create a digital weapon, governments take apart popular computer systems such as Microsoft Windows, find their flaws, weaponize those flaws, and release those weapons on their own or to allies.

For example, a flaw in Windows might allow someone to infect a Windows-based computer. Delivering a piece of malicious code this way can give the cyberattacker full remote control of that computer silently. Because the criminals do this in secret, Microsoft doesn't know to release a fix for the flaw. This means that a nation-state or government can, at the touch of a button, deliver a digital munition that allows them to control or disable every computer they can reach over the Internet and share that control with any friends or allies to do whatever they wish. In the case of some of the biggest cyberattacks in recent memory, they can also delete data and destroy systems.

Giving someone like Bogachev a digital weapon is the modern equivalent of equipping a rebel group with AK-47s or weaponized germs: the arms might serve the nation's intended purpose in the short term, but in the long term, who knows what the rebel like Bogachev will do with those weapons or who he'll use them on.

And just like the threat of nuclear weapons has proliferated in recent decades, the deliberate or accidental release of virulent cyberweapons poses increasingly greater risks to everyone.

Some nation-states and cybercriminals such as Bogachev will deploy their digital weapons for surveillance purposes. They can use them to monitor a company's deals and intellectual property, then sell that information over the Dark Web or perform economic espionage. This kind of surveillance allows cybercriminals to know you go on long trips, how you write your emails and when, and whom you typically communicate with. This is what allows cybercriminals to conduct their phishing attacks with such precision. Understand that as a business executive, you are a major target for this kind of silent surveillance.

## WEBSITE GRAFFITI AND SMALL-TIME HACKTIVISTS

Why does this activity vary so drastically from our previous perceptions of cybercriminals? In short, because our perceptions of cybercriminals were formed during a much simpler time for mischief on the Internet.

Before organized crime made its way online, one of the biggest forms of trouble people caused on the Internet was defacing websites. Online activists (or hacktivists, which means a "hacker with a political agenda") would break into company or government websites and change page content to promote their agenda. Most often, hacktivists wanted to use a company's web property to defame them. If hacktivists had a larger, global agenda, they might have targeted certain websites simply because they wanted to take advantage of an entity's web presence to publish the hacktivists' manifesto.

One of the most prominent agenda-driven hacktivist events in recent memory is the release of the Panama Papers. Rich and powerful people hide their assets in offshore accounts to evade taxes. It's been a well-known and common practice for decades. It just so happens that there was a single clearinghouse that facilitated the biggest and shadiest offshore accounts in the world. That clearinghouse was a Panamanian law firm called Mossack Fonseca, and in 2016 they were exposed...by a single, politically driven hacktivist.

Rather than seeking personal gain, this individual (known only as "John Doe") was intent on striking a blow against global income inequality. That's unusual. Even more unusual? The amount of damage the Panama Papers caused *greatly* outweighed the effort it took to leak them. The papers named heads of state and royalty as offshore account holders. Never before in human history has one person with so few resources inflicted that much damage in the name of their agenda.

The hacktivist had access to Mossack Fonseca's data for *eighteen months*. It wasn't even an incredibly difficult tech hack. If a hacker from 1995 had been cryogenically frozen and woke up in 2015, they could have hacked that law firm. And still, firm management had no idea.

You could look at the Panama Papers as an example of bad people who deserved to be exposed. That's fair. But as an executive for a successful and, presumably, ethical company, you should take this as a cautionary tale: most cybercriminals are amoral, and if they desire, they could hack you in the same way.

## PRIME MINISTER BEAN

Or sometimes hacktivists just want to have fun. For example, in 2010 hackers took control of the European Union's website and replaced the photo of the prime minister with an image of Mr. Bean.

Small-time vandals and hacktivists are annoying, but they're not the main driver of the $6 trillion of annual global damages estimated by 2021. Hollywood portrayals of computer hacking and cybercrimes have been predicated on this perception of harmlessness.

One of my favorite examples of a cybersecurity breach portrayed in pop culture is the 1983 movie *War Games*. In the movie, Matthew Broderick plays a curious teenager with disengaged parents and professional-grade computer gear retrieved from dumpsters. Bored with school and looking for ways to play games on his computer, he unknowingly hacks into the Department of Defense computer in control of nuclear missiles. In the process, he accidentally starts a program called Thermonuclear War, which he thinks is a game, but actually gives him the power to launch nuclear weapons and start World War III.

The modern equivalent of *War Games* is a TV show called *Mr. Robot*. In *Mr. Robot*, the protagonist is yet another lonely, socially disengaged young man, except in this popular culture portrayal, the protagonist is a vigilante. He catches small-time criminals online, then turns them in to the police, all while committing crimes himself, such as using illicit drugs, aiding and abetting a gang of hacktivists bringing down the economy, and committing virtually every computer crime for which we have a law.

From watching these pop culture representations of hackers and cybercriminals, it's no wonder the public has this perception that the Internet is full of nothing more than anklebiters—the types of activists that would turn a prime minister's face into Mr. Bean.

But that perception is only a small part of the full story. Cybercriminals are capable of much more damage. They could even shut down your entire business.

## BOGACHEV'S SMILE ZONE ATTACK

On East Sunshine Street in Springfield, Missouri, is a pediatric dentist's office called Smile Zone. Smile Zone's philosophy is to ease children's fears about going to the dentist. They believe that children should be given all the time they need in order to become comfortable with every dental procedure they perform.

They operated within a specific philosophy that guided every interaction they had with parents and children. Unfortunately, like many businesses—big and small— they didn't have a clear set of cybersecurity policies and procedures, which left them vulnerable to a cyberattack. They were a dentist's office. Cybersecurity was one of the last business threats on their minds. But it still came back to harm their company. Their biggest mistake was falling for a silent phishing attack on the computer they used to conduct their bank transactions.

In 2010, Bogachev created a piece of malicious code that one of his minions got onto that personal computer. Bogachev's gang member remotely monitored Smile Zone's transactions for several weeks in order to learn their banking habits. Then, when the time was right, Bogachev used the dentist's valid credentials to steal $205,000 from Smile Zone's checking account. The Smile Zone, a dentist for children, never recovered that money.

Once a cybercriminal takes money, it's incredibly difficult to recover. In the case of Smile Zone, there was a combination of factors that prevented them from getting their money back. One factor was that the money was stolen from a commercial checking account, which operates under a different set of rules and regulations than consumer accounts. For example, consumer accounts enjoy extremely limited liabilities. Most major credit card companies and issuing banks offer zero liability protection to consumers. In other words, if a thief uses your account to make purchases, you're not liable for a penny of the charges, no matter how big the fraud. Commercial accounts have no such protection.

The other factor that kept Smile Zone from recovering their money was that from the bank's point of view, the transaction that moved money out of Smile Zone's bank account was a perfectly valid transaction. It had all the authenticity markers of any other transaction that had been performed on that personal computer over the years prior. Therefore, the bank assumed no liability for the loss.

You might look at a pediatric dentist's office as a strange target for a cyberattack, but that's a major misconception. Small businesses are prime targets. Because they don't have as much cash flow as a large corporation, they don't defend themselves against cyberattacks with the same level of sophistication as a big business. As a result, criminals cast a wide net very cheaply, just to see how many small businesses they can hack.

In fact, the cost of committing a crime like the one pulled on Smile Zone is much lower than you would think. A cybercriminal in Eastern Europe could pay a hacker just a few dollars a day to attack small businesses in the West. With that overhead, a $205,000 theft after several weeks of reconnaissance and study is a highly profitable activity, even if it took dozens of failed hacks to get one success.

## THE BULLY WANTS YOU TO COME BACK TOMORROW

The fact that the fraudulent transactions were fully formed and legitimate is incredibly important. They didn't want to put Smile Zone out of business with one big hack. They wanted to take their money slowly, without detection, so they could come back for more the next day. Just like the bully who stole your milk money every day in grade school, the hacker doesn't want to beat you up so bad you have to drop out of school. They need your milk money every day. So even if they threaten you and scream at you, they're counting on you coming back the next day with more money for them to take. Bogachev's attacker could have stolen more than that $205,000 from Smile Zone, but they didn't because their end goal was not to put them out of business. It was to take large amounts of money over time.

Even after Smile Zone realized they were being pilfered, nobody could help them—not the bank, law enforcement, the military, or the judicial system. Some day in the future, small businesses in America will be able to count on banks and government agencies to do a better job preventing these kinds of cyberattacks. But that day is still fifteen to twenty years away, or more.

In the Western world, especially here in the United States, we are accustomed to being protected from criminals. And when a crime is successful, we are accustomed to receiving justice for the transgressions that were committed against us. Unfortunately, the same institutions that protect us from physical theft are incapable of protecting us from digital theft, except in the most extraordinary, heroic circumstances. For now, at least, you're on your own, and that can be a scary change to accept.

## MACHINE GUNS TO NUCLEAR
## BOMBS TO CYBERWEAPONS

This change is the historical equivalent to the emergence of the machine gun-toting bank robber in 1930s America. Like cyberattackers today, the gangsters used a combination of new technologies, such as handheld machine guns, to overwhelm law enforcement. It took sixty years for the FBI and banks to figure out how to neutralize bank branch robbery threats. It required a combination of new laws, new police technologies (e.g., radios and bulletproof vests), and new bank branch practices (e.g., limiting cash on hand, silent alarms, and video cameras).

Likewise, our governing bodies' struggle to handle cyberthreats is similar to the struggles we faced during the rise of nuclear weapons. Nuclear weapons were introduced in 1945. Even into the 1980s, we were still trying to figure out how to regulate the use of nuclear weapons. When was their use justified? How could we establish norms around their production? Who deserved to have them? Those were the questions we grappled with.

Even today, with Iran and North Korea, we still struggle to affect a sense of governance over the possession, creation, and use of nuclear weapons. The rise of cyberweapons is on the same scale as those two major changes in our society in the twentieth century. But given the nature of digital technologies, they are also unlike anything we've seen before.

We're used to living in a society that is highly governed by the rule of law and provides a healthy structure within which you can conduct your business. Cyber risks take you out of that structure and place you in a log cabin in the middle of nowhere. We are pioneers in the digital landscape. There are no fire hydrants, no police, no 911, no military, and no insurance—fire or otherwise. All of these structures we're used to in the real world are either missing in cyberspace or are infantile in their capabilities. The only way to opt out of cyber risk is to disconnect from the Internet, and no twenty-first-century business can afford to do that.

## CODE SPACES

At its height, Code Spaces was a cloud services provider with more than two hundred customers. In short, they provided data storage where companies could host their programs, files, and software. They were successful—emphasis on *were*.

In 2014, the owners and executives of Code Spaces received an email from cybercriminals saying they had taken control of the company's computers, and they wouldn't return control to the owners until they received a ransom. Code Spaces' executives were tech-savvy and did the right thing by refusing to pay the ransom.

Instead, they attempted to regain control of their systems. When the attackers saw the attempted recovery, they proceeded to erase everything, destroying all of the systems. Every company program and every scrap of data—either belonging to the company and its employees, or to its customers—was erased. The cost of rapid recovery was completely out of reach for Code Spaces.

They went bankrupt within a week.

These kinds of cyberattacks aren't carried out by ankle biters or lonely kids looking to switch the prime minister's face with Mr. Bean. They are carried out by sophisticated criminal organizations so nefarious that your entire business can be swept out from underneath you at a moment's notice, no matter how smart or tech-savvy you are.

## THE CLOUD IS JUST SOMEONE ELSE'S COMPUTER

Just because cloud vendors tell you that it's more secure to do your business on the cloud doesn't automatically make it so. Just look at Code Space. Their customers who didn't have separate backups lost everything.

Simply put, the cloud is just someone else's computer. It's easy to be swept up in the belief that it's more complex than that, but it really isn't. Granted, Amazon, Microsoft, and Google all have cloud services with complex features, and they are the peak of sophistication when it comes to keeping their systems running, but at the end of the day, putting your files onto their clouds is just using their computers as your storage.

People who talk about the cloud in more complicated ways are ignorant, have an agenda, or both. Most often, they want you to buy something from them, so they ramp up your fear by making it sound more complicated than it really is. They're like car mechanics who suggest repairs that sound so complicated they just bank on you agreeing to them out of sheer mental fatigue.

As a business executive today, your security goals need to be different than they used to be. Your goal used to be preventing people from stealing your assets, digital or physical. The majority of your spending was prevention-oriented. That was OK in the past, but that's not going to be sufficient in the future.

We've developed nearly perfect prevention and response measures for fires. Fire doesn't innovate, so once we figured out how it works, we were able to develop strategies to prevent further damage going forward. There is no perfect prevention for the Bogachevs of the world. As we move toward a more cybercentric future, your cybersecurity policy needs to be based on the assumption that you will be breached. No matter how hard you work to prevent it, cybercriminals are so competent, capable, well resourced, innovative, and well equipped that they will get you eventually.

The question you now have to answer is, "How will you recover when you are breached?"

# CYBER RISK
# MANAGEMENT

In April 2017, a hacker group called the Shadow Brokers leaked a previously unknown exploit in Microsoft Windows onto the Dark Web. The exploit was developed by the US National Security Agency (NSA), who gave it the code name EternalBlue. And, in a prime example of cyberweapon proliferation, someone stole it, and it fell into the hands of the Shadow Brokers. The Shadow Brokers are an anonymous cybercriminal group that spends their time antagonizing the US government by leaking sensitive information designed to make it look incompetent.

But earlier in 2017, the NSA expected EternalBlue would be released to the public, so they gave Microsoft advanced notice. And on March 14, 2017, one month before the public release of EternalBlue, Microsoft issued a security bulletin. It detailed the EternalBlue flaw and announced that security updates had been released.

At the same time the Shadow Brokers unleashed their knowledge of the EternalBlue exploit into the wild of the Dark Web, another hacker group compromised the source code of a popular Ukrainian tax software package. It was the equivalent of Quicken for Ukrainians, and it held an 80 percent market share for tax software. Because of its wide distribution, this second hacker group saw a perfect opportunity. They could use the Eternal-Blue exploit to unleash a malicious code that eventually became known as NotPetya. So they hacked into the tax company's servers and inserted NotPetya into the company's software package.

Later analysis of the servers for the exploited Ukrainian tax software showed that security updates had not been applied since 2013. Also, an M.E. Doc employee's account on the servers had been compromised, and there was evidence of a Russian presence.

Without knowing their update had been weaponized, the company inadvertently released it to their customers as part of their normal update cycle. In other words, the company themselves unwittingly fired the weapon.

**DIGITAL WEAPONS**

Think of digital weapons as highly effective viruses: they are little packages of malicious code that find weak spots in a system and attack them. Viruses make humans sick, and digital weapons (which are also called viruses) make computers sick or even completely stop working. In the same way a single sick person in a social circle can infect the entire group, a single sick computer can infect the entire network. Because the NotPetya code was launched on a large scale, the effects were more likely to be widespread.

At first, people thought NotPetya was ransomware. When it infected someone's computer, a full screen of text appeared saying:

```
Ooops, your important files are encrypted.

If you see this text, then your files are no longer accessible, because they
have been encrypted. Perhaps you are busy looking for a way to recover your
files, but don't waste your time. Nobody can recover your files without our
decryption service.

We guarantee that you can recover all your files safely and easily. All you
need to do is submit the payment and purchase the decryption key.

Please follow the instructions:

1. Send $300 worth of Bitcoin to following address:

    1Mz7                                    BWX

2. Send your Bitcoin wallet ID and personal installation key to e-mail
   wowsmith123456@posteo.net. Your personal installation key:

    NJJH                                                        P5

If you already purchased your key, please enter it below.
Key:
```

It was later discovered that this was merely a misdirection. The true purpose of the weapon was to simply delete as much data on the computer as possible and render it unusable. But note: Windows users had more than *ninety days* to install the security update that neutralized NotPetya, and the people who were victimized never installed that update.

## THE EFFECTS OF NOTPETYA

Maersk is the largest container shipping company in the world. They own enormous cargo container ships and operate shipping ports all around the world: Amsterdam, Los Angeles, Hong Kong, New Jersey, Alabama, India, and Spain, to name just a few. Maersk had computers everywhere that were infected by NotPetya, which resulted in a massive slowdown of their operations. It was so bad that they couldn't accept every new shipment offered to them, and they didn't know where many of the existing shipments were. Many of their ports had to revert back to pen and paper just to be able to operate.

In Mobile, Alabama, the longshoremen had to load and unload containers manually.

In Port Elizabeth, New Jersey, they had to shut down all shipping for days.

In the end, after just one quarter, Maersk lost $300 million because of NotPetya. They did not have a framework in place to help them prevent or recover, and they continue to feel the negative impact today.

The White House called NotPetya "the costliest cyber-attack in history" and blamed it on the Russian military. They estimated the total global private sector losses at $10 billion.

## ONE COMPANY THAT DID IT RIGHT

TNT, a subsidiary of FedEx, also experienced negative side effects of NotPetya. For weeks, they couldn't deliver or receive package orders. They had giant warehouses stuffed to the ceilings with tens of thousands of packages whose destinations they didn't know because the computer systems that track that information weren't available. They had no cyberinsurance to help them absorb their losses, which totaled more than half a billion dollars.

FedEx's European competitor, DHL, was also hit by NotPetya. Unlike FedEx—which suffered tremendously—DHL hardly took any losses. Because DHL had good cybersecurity recovery practices in place, including prompt installation of updates, they were able to withstand the attack. While we don't know how DHL handled the attack internally, we do know that their financial bottom line and their growing shipment volumes immediately following the attack reflect their resilience. Their cyberresilience turned into a competitive advantage for them.

## CYBERWAR: WHAT DOES IT MEAN FOR YOUR BUSINESS?

NotPetya exposed just how unprepared most companies are for cyberattacks. As an executive, you have no way of knowing when a foreign government, a lone cybercriminal, or even *your own* government will release or mishandle a cyberweapon. Therefore, you have to prepare for the possibility of attack in much the same way you would prepare your business for other unexpected events, such as hurricanes and earthquakes.

You can't predict when a natural disaster will strike, nor

should you live in fear of their occurrence. Your best practice is to be proactive in creating a cyber risk management program so that when disaster strikes, your company is still in business.

## THE FOUR CYLINDERS OF CYBER RISK MANAGEMENT

A good cyber risk management program is like a four-cylinder car engine. You count on all four pistons firing in order and on time to give you the power you need to drive your company. If any of those cylinders is out of sync, your entire journey is unbalanced. In cyber risk management, those cylinders are people, process, management, and technology. Each one is just as important as the other, but they each pose unique obstacles in protecting your company from cyberattacks like NotPetya.

### PEOPLE

If your people are too technologically dependent and your computer systems go down, they will no longer operate as efficiently as possible. People will have to scramble. They will work harder and longer trying to invent ways to manually accomplish what they used to do with technology. Look at what happened with Maersk: they went to using pen and paper when their computer systems went down. This led to inconsistencies because their process was not standardized. Without the people cylinder firing properly, you will have a group of *individuals* each operating without consistency.

Erie County Medical Center in Buffalo was hit with a piece of ransomware in 2017 that wiped out their computer systems for weeks. They chose not to pay the ransom, which was the right choice, but it cost them $10 million to recover from the attack. When they did recover, they had stacks of inconsistent, manually created medical records that they had to reinput into their system. All because their people were not prepared for a cyberattack.

**WHY YOU SHOULD NEVER PAY A RANSOM**

When one person pays a ransom to a cybercriminal, they are voting for more cyberattacks. Erie County Medical Center was threatened for $55,000 in ransom, but they wound up paying $10 million to recover. Of course they should pay the $55,000 ransom, right? Why in the world would they pay $10 million when they could get off for 0.5 percent of that? Because paying the ransom says to criminals everywhere, "We are willing to pay you money if you can compromise our systems. Please come back again soon!" Paying the ransom emboldens criminals and puts a target on your back, which may cost you more in the long run. It also encourages cyberattacks against everyone in our online community, and that's bad for all businesses.

Oddly enough, cybercriminals have a reputation for keeping their word. In fact, some are renowned for their superior customer service. If they request to be paid in Bitcoin, they will provide a phone number in the ransomware dialog box where you can talk to someone on the phone as they walk you through acquiring Bitcoin and paying the ransom. There are entire offices across the world dedicated to operations like this. They're not a bunch of bored teenagers in their mothers' basements. These are corporations with employees, payrolls, and a very real incentive for exploiting you.

## PROCESS

If you don't have robust processes documented, people won't know how to get their work done without the aid of technology. Lack of process leads to inconsistent results during a cyberattack. Without a process, your employees only create additional problems. In the case of Erie County Medical Center, a lack of documented process could result in not delivering adequate care, which could lead to patients getting hurt, which of course opens them up to lawsuits.

One way to mitigate the procedural risk of a cyberattack is to keep hard copies of your company's procedures on hand so that you can use manual procedures at a moment's notice, for an indefinite period. Your processes should be thorough. In the medical facility, for example, they should have had a physical checklist to ensure the medical staff followed the necessary steps to ensure patients received their full, necessary treatments.

By not providing these processes for people, you're leaving the health of your company up to chance. In Erie County Medical Center's case, the safest route would have been to stop seeing patients, in much the same way FedEx and Maersk stopped accepting new shipments. If you're ever forced to make that choice, it will permanently harm your business.

The most reliable way to put this into practice is to go old school: keep your manual processes—with preprinted forms—in three-ring binders, and use pens, pencils, and paper. In the case of the medical facility, one innovative thing they did was have the staff use their own phones and personal computers when the company computers went down. Normally this would increase the cyber risks they faced, but the medical center had been securely sharing its medical records with a clearinghouse, so they were able to arrange for their doctors and nurses to access those records securely from their personal devices.

It's important to practice these emergency cyberattack procedures the same way you'd run a fire drill. Choose a department in your company and pretend something horrible has happened and they have to do everything offline. Ask them: "Can you get your work done using these alternate manual procedures?" See what they're able to accomplish without the aid of technology, and use that information to help build out your cyberattack processes.

Another important aspect to your business processes is making sure they are strong enough to resist an exploitation by a cyberattacker. The business email compromise attack relies, in large part, on funds transfer processes that permit large sums of money to move on the strength of a single, terse email, and the too quick response of an overwhelmed person in the accounting or finance departments.

You should speak with your bank to find out how to strengthen controls over the electronic movement of large amounts of your money. A common technique is called dual authorization. This safeguard requires authorization from two people from the same business to complete a large payment electronically. One person creates a payment request (the originator), and the other authorizes the payment (the authorizer). While this extra step slows down your payments, it will also detect a lot of attempts to steal your money, by both internal and external people.

## MANAGEMENT

It is management's responsibility to know that cyber risks exist and to create and test plans that are designed to keep the organization running if these risks materialize. If management doesn't create three-ring binders with preprinted forms, or cardboard cash registers, or find alternate ways to access records off-line, then it's your failure as an executive.

Management is a cylinder, but it's also the master computer inside the car. The computer contained in every car that controls how well the engine runs can turn cylinders on and off to save fuel, and can decide what the fuel mixture should be when the engine is operating. Without that master controller—management—there is chaos and mayhem. The engine can't run, or it runs in such a shoddy way that it won't meet your needs or will damage itself.

You don't have to be a cyber risk expert or a technological whiz to become a good cyber risk manager. In fact, when technology fails, all the technological expertise in the world will not help you. As a leader, you have to anticipate a technology failure and run your business without it.

## TECHNOLOGY

When I say that technology is one of the cylinders of your cyber risk management plan, I don't mean you have to understand all of the bits and bytes of your company's tech. Not at all. What you do have to understand is exactly *how* technology can fail you and how to be prepared for those failures with no advance notice.

You should focus on ensuring you have a reasonable cybersecurity framework so that you can identify the major risks to your digital assets. Prevention is important, but in case something bad does happen, you need to detect the compromise, respond to it, and recover as quickly as possible. That is what you need to be focused on with regard to technology, rather than becoming an expert in technology itself.

How do you ensure your company is running all four cylinders—people, process, management, and technology—as smoothly as possible? By using something known as the National Institute of Standards of Technology (NIST) Cybersecurity Framework.

## THE NIST CYBERSECURITY FRAMEWORK

The US government has recognized that the Internet is becoming increasingly dangerous for all Americans due to the activities of organized crime and foreign nation-states. They also recognize that our country's critical infrastructure all depends on computers, which includes electrical power generation and distribution, natural gas procurement and distribution, the ability to deliver clean drinking water to homes, the ability to remove solid wastes and sewage from homes and businesses, telephone services, and Internet connectivity.

And the federal government has realized that they can't be everywhere to protect all of this infrastructure or the private businesses that provide the services dependent on computers, so they wanted to enable organizations and citizens in the United States to protect themselves. As a result, they produced a framework that anyone can use in order to be more prepared for cyberattacks.

As you review the NIST Framework below, keep in mind that we're approaching cyber risk as a business problem, not just a technological one. While you will see many technological aspects in the framework, it will take initiative on the part of your executive leadership to make sure all aspects of the framework are carefully considered and adopted in light of your people, processes, management, and technology.

The five-function NIST Framework is an incredibly adaptive and ingenious solution. It's not prescriptive. Rather than tell people exactly what to do, the framework gives businesses like yours the information you need to come up with your own effective cybersecurity plans tailored to your specific business.

The framework is organized around five functions:

- Identify
- Protect

- Detect
- Respond
- Recover

All five functions must be executed contemporaneously and should be done at a certain minimum level of effectiveness.

## IDENTIFY

Identifying your assets and risks is foundational to your ability to execute the rest of the steps in the NIST Cybersecurity Framework. If you're overlooking any asset—including your customers' credit card information, for example—then you won't know if you have the right protection and detective controls in place.

In 2009, the FTC (Federal Trade Commission) accused CVS Pharmacy of not having any cybersecurity policies. For a pharmacy, it was a harsh claim. They oversee a lot of sensitive data from their customers. So surely, they had a structured, systematic, comprehensive process in place to protect that private data, right? No. Not only did they not have a comprehensive process, they didn't have any process. It was off their radar completely. As such, the FTC found that CVS was putting their customers' health care at risk by not securing their sensitive data.

Another great example of this is the Health Insurance Portability and Accountability Act (HIPAA) of 1996, which requires that anyone in possession of an electronic health care record protects that record according to HIPAA's specifications. However, many companies carry sensitive digital assets for which there are no external compliance regulations, such as payroll records and trade secrets.

Ironically, if you're too focused on complying with outside regulators, you won't be effective in protecting all of your digital assets. You will maintain only the bare minimum of compliance without identifying your less obvious risks and assets. What you need is a comprehensive, prioritized inventory of all of your assets, where they are, who's handling them, and who's been granted access to them. If third parties have access to your sensitive digital assets, you need to make sure they're exercising the same caution that you would in the processing and storing of that data.

Without identifying your assets, and the risks to them, you won't be able to protect them.

## PROTECT

The Protect step is based in the idea that after having identified your assets and your risks, you can now take action to prevent bad things from happening to them.

You know which assets to protect, and this framework contains a tremendous amount of material on the different ways that you can do that. You can implement access control so that people who are not authorized to access an asset are blocked from doing so. You can also educate people and train them on how to avoid common security risks, such as a phishing attack. There are also techniques such as data encryption (which we will discuss later) to prevent attackers from looking at your data even if they happen to come into possession of it.

Your goal is to have the correct processes and procedures in place, such as backing up the data on your systems, and conducting a test to make sure that the data that you've backed up can, in fact, be restored. You would not believe how many times people have been doing data backups for years, then, when something really horrible happened and they tried to restore their data from the backups, they found that their backup system never worked, and they didn't know because they never tested it.

## NEGATIVE VISUALIZATION

As an executive, you need to cultivate a habit called negative visualization. Most people don't practice this because it is emotionally difficult when you first start. It can be a disturbing practice. Negative visualization is when you imagine what it would be like if you lost something that you highly value. Most executives happily engage in positive visualization. They say, "When we land that next customer, we're going to have a wonderful quarter!" They are always thinking about good things that they want to happen, but they don't spend enough time visualizing what will happen if something goes wrong. By engaging in a regular practice of negative visualization, you can open your mind to the possibilities that the NIST Cybersecurity Framework is designed to help you manage.

Say an executive just allocated a large sum of money to purchase a system that would automatically back up their sensitive data so they can restore it at a moment's notice. If they are not participating in negative visualization, they don't ask themselves the question, "What if my system doesn't actually restore the data that we've been backing up, and how can I make sure the system works correctly?" If they do ask themselves that question, they may then say, "I know! I can run a test every quarter, randomly selecting a file that I want my team to restore so they can show me they can do it."

This is what I mean when I say you don't need to be a technological expert to be a good cybersecurity risk manager. You don't need to know *why* the data backup system might fail; you only need to imagine that possibility.

DETECT

Simply put, detection is your ability to recognize when something bad has happened to your digital assets. It takes, on average, anywhere between one hundred to two hundred days for someone to know they've suffered a data breach. By that time, you may not be able to recover whatever has been lost, including your and your customers' sensitive data. Most executives don't have a specific set of practices to help them detect cyberattacks. They often find out through a third party.

There are actually three specific ways that most executives discover they've been breached:

1. Law enforcement contacts them unexpectedly. This usually happens when officials discover a stash of data while investigating a different crime.
2. A customer or business partner calls them and says, "I trusted you with my sensitive data, but it was stolen from you. Now you have to pay for the repercussions."
3. A news reporter contacts them. They say something to the effect of, "We've just learned that your company has suffered a massive data breach, and we've prepared a story. We're going to release it on the five o'clock news. Would you care to comment before we make the story live?"

A wise executive makes it a point to detect when breaches happen within their organization without needing an outsider to tell them. A long detection time means law enforcement, customers, and media have a longer time frame to convict you in the court of public opinion. Moreover, the longer it takes for you to detect a breach, the higher the cost will be for you to respond to it.

## RESPOND

Perfect prevention of all cybersecurity breaches is no longer possible. That's why responses are built into the NIST Framework. After you find out about a breach, your goal is to contain the damage. Ensure you have a marvelous communications plan prepared and practiced. That includes which of your stakeholders you'll inform and at what priority. Likewise, make sure you have a public relations person to distribute press releases and handle media queries as professionally as possible.

Moreover, talk to a lawyer who can interpret the different statutes that apply to your situation, *then* you'll notify law enforcement. The first time you call law enforcement should not be the moment your hair is on fire because of the recent data breach. In fact, once you develop your cyber risk management game plan, you should be in contact with law enforcement—before you need them—to let them know what your plan is. This will not only make them more prepared when you do push the red panic button, but they will also give you the benefit of the doubt when you do.

**CYBERINSURANCE**

Someone who is good at negative visualization will see many of the ways something can go wrong in the future. That means they'll have thoughtfully considered earthquake insurance, umbrella insurance, life insurance, flood insurance, and, of course, fire insurance. For you, the information in this book should help you consider a different kind of insurance: cyberinsurance. Nevertheless, the ability to productively engage in negative visualization will help you anticipate, guard against, and respond to cyberbreaches in the future.

In the world of yesterday, company reputations were rarely severely damaged because of cybersecurity risks. In the world we live in today—and the world we will live in tomorrow—it's almost a guarantee that you will experience a costly cyberbreach. Cyberinsurance can be a good tool to manage the negative impact of that inevitability.

If you read this book and follow the advice contained herein, you will be prepared to respond to a data breach, but you actually have to follow through on it. It's easy to say that you'll have a prewritten press release for a cybersecurity breach, but it's another thing entirely to actually execute on that plan.

Find competent people who have experience guiding an organization through a data breach response. Those are the people you should have on your team, whether you hire them or contract them (depending on your risk levels). As an executive, there is no need to feel that you have to respond to a data breach alone. Quite the opposite. You won't contain the damage of a data breach without a team of prepared professionals ready to respond and recover.

One of the best ways to build a response team is to buy a cyber resilience insurance policy that offers a data breach coach along with on-demand response services, such as:

- Digital forensics
- Crisis communications
- Legal defense
- Data breach notification

## RECOVER

Once you have successfully contained a cybersecurity incident and it is no longer causing damage to you or your stakeholders, your major focus shifts to recovery. In general, you can begin recovery activities before you've mitigated the incident—there is some overlap—but it's easier to think of these as distinct steps in the framework. The goal of the Recover phase is to make sure that, similar to the Erie County Medical Center, you can return to normal operations as quickly and as securely as possible. That not only includes the operational aspects of your organization but also the public relations side. Once you have achieved some level of recovery, you can open your doors and declare that the incident has been handled.

This is why it is vital to be proactive about public relations in the Respond phase. Just because your doors are open doesn't mean your customers will walk through them. Your reputation is everything. The court of public opinion can put you out of business in a flash if you let it. People will move to your competitors the same way FedEx customers moved to DHL after the NotPetya attack.

If your customers do leave, getting them to return is a function of the Recover phase. You have to engage in dialogue with them. Explain to them—in simple terms—what has happened, how sorry you are, and what steps you've taken to ensure this won't happen again in the future.

## HACKING BACK—ETHICAL OR NOT?

If your digital assets have been stolen, whether it's money or data, part of the Recover function will consist of recovering those sensitive assets and neutralizing the thief's ability to exploit what they stole. This function leads us into an emergent option called hacking back. The conversation around hacking back is very new but very energetic. It's a hotly debated topic. Do companies have the right to take back what was stolen from them in the first place? The governor of Georgia doesn't think so. Governor Nathan Deal vetoed a piece of legislation in 2018 that would have allowed companies to hack back if they are attacked.

However, in 2017, Representative Tom Graves, a Republican from Georgia, submitted a bill to the House that proposed to legalize several measures currently prohibited by the Computer Fraud and Abuse Act. According to the bill, private firms would be permitted to operate beyond their network's perimeter in order to determine the source of an attack or to disrupt ongoing attacks. In other words, the bill would allow hacking back.

There's not a lot of clarity on this issue, but this is the most important thing: hacking back is currently illegal and potentially unethical. Why unethical? Because any hacker with a brain would not attack you from their own personal computer. They always attack through someone else's computer. If you hack back and are not able to take that into consideration, you could hack an innocent victim, just like yourself.

My take: rather than hack back, you should explore less risky but more effective forms of active defense. One example is the "honeypot," a tool that attracts hackers to decoy servers, where they can be diverted, slowed down, and monitored to gather intelligence on hacker behavior.

*Into the Gray Zone* is an easy-to-read, free report on various forms of active defense from the George Washington University Center for Cyber and Homeland Security. It's a great resource that you can download here: http://b.link/activedefense.

## CYBERSECURITY IS A JOURNEY

Imagine a man hanging off the side of a moving train. He's probably enjoying his journey from point A to point B, and he's likely spending no money doing it. After all, he didn't have to buy a ticket. Despite his carefree attitude, he's choosing an extremely risky form of travel. All he's thinking about is how to get to his destination and totally disregarding his safety during the journey.

In your business, your destination is more revenue, more profits, and better customers. Just like the man hanging off the side of the train, if your train runs into an obstacle you don't expect—such as a cow on the tracks (or a major cybersecurity breach)—it might knock the entire train off the rails, causing harm to everyone inside who paid for their tickets, especially you hanging off the side. But if the obstacle is small, such as a narrow tunnel (or a minor ransomware attack), it might be just enough to knock you off the side while those who prepared and paid for their journey will experience nothing more than a light bounce.

You have to ask yourself how well protected you are from an attack and how well you *want to be protected* for the attack. Are you hanging off the side of the train, living cheaply but dangerously? Or did you spend a little bit of money to ride inside the train? Maybe you only need coach tickets because you're a smaller organization. Or maybe you're a bank and you need to pony up the money to sit in first class. It's much safer, and you're more likely to get to your destination on time and in one piece.

That's the most important lesson to remember: cybersecurity isn't a destination; it's a journey. And the quality of your journey depends on the choices you make. Do all four cylinders of your company—the people, processes, management, and technology—all fire in unison to get you to your destination? If they're not, you should take a look at the five functions of the NIST Cybersecurity Framework to help you better identify your cyber risks, protect against them, detect breaches when they do happen (because perfect prevention is impossible), respond to them, and recover as quickly and as professionally as possible. In fact, we'll do this in part 2 of this book.

You get to decide how much you want to spend—in both effort and time—with cybersecurity. You can protect your assets at a minimal level for the kind of business you are and the type of data you possess, or at a world class level, or anywhere in between. Whatever you choose should be a conscious decision based on what's best for your organization and reasonable as defined by the FTC. Otherwise, you'll leave yourself open to viruses as big and as disruptive as NotPetya.

How do you protect yourself from cyber risks on the

journey to your goals? You practice what I call good cyberhygiene.

# GERM THEORY AND CYBERHYGIENE

For most of human history, people had no idea why they got sick. The main villain for hundreds of years was "bad air." It wasn't until relatively recently that we discovered the invisible organisms we now know as germs. Because their transmission from person to person is a common way that illness is spread, we have learned to wash our hands, cover our mouths when we cough or sneeze, and get a flu shot annually. We all take these precautions in response to being told germs exist, even though none of us has ever seen one with the naked eye.

You can think of cyberattackers and the risks they pose to your sensitive data in much the same way. You rarely see your attackers, and you can't see the viruses they spread before they got to you, which makes them easier to ignore. But they can still hurt you.

We accept that germs can make us sick, and we're even willing to inconvenience ourselves to practice good hygiene on a daily, weekly, monthly, and even annual basis to guard against them. Similarly, in order to stave off digital "germs" and viruses, you have to partake in regularly scheduled hygienic practices to protect both you and your company.

> If you want to be as healthy as possible, you visit an expert to catch and treat diseases before they become serious. For your personal health, that expert is your doctor. For your cybersecurity health, that expert is me.

Here are some of the most important digital "handwashing" techniques to practice good cyberhygiene.

## DON'T USE AN ADMIN ACCOUNT FOR EVERYDAY BUSINESS ACTIVITIES

In 1995, a single person brought down one of the United Kingdom's oldest banks. This wasn't a cyberattack either. The man was *employed* by the bank.

Nick Leeson was a futures trader for London-based Barings Bank, which, at the time of its collapse, had been in operation for more than 230 years. Nick had limited authorization to make trades for the company, and there were certain measures in place to ensure he never exceeded his mandate.

Barings Bank required all of its traders to report their losses and gains on a regular basis to ensure none of them suffered excessive losses at the cost of the company. Nick, however, had too much access to the company computer systems, which conducted trades and kept records of all gains and losses.

Nick took advantage of his privileged access to the company's internal auditing system. He did his work each day—making trades and harvesting gains or losses—then went into the computer and hid his tracks.

Why did he have to hide his tracks? Because his risk appetite far exceeded the conservative bank he worked for, so Nick's trades ran amok: he consistently took major losses on risky trades. Through his deceit, Nick covered up more than $1 billion in his trading losses and ultimately put Barings Bank out of business.

He was eventually caught and sentenced to prison, but he got away with it for as long as he did because the bank executives' preventive and detective procedures were not effective enough. The system to manage their traders' losses and gains was a worthless internal auditing tool if one of the traders themselves had access to that system.

## RISK APPETITES

Every organization has a risk appetite. In other words, your company has a certain level of risky behavior that it's willing to accept in order to make a profit or achieve a social or government mission. Likewise, people within the organization each have their own individual risk appetites. Therefore, as an executive, your first step to preventing the Nick Leesons of the world from sabotaging your company is recognizing, then communicating, your organization's risk appetite.

## LOW-RISK APPETITE

An insurance company is an example of a low-risk appetite company. Insurance is a highly regulated industry, so state auditors keep insurance companies from taking outsized financial risks with their customers' money. Through regular state-mandated audits, an insurance company is always certain they have enough money in their reserves to pay for customer claims. They also have insurance policies in case of catastrophic losses. In other words, it's not only in the company's best interest to maintain a low-risk appetite, but they are also required to do so.

## MEDIUM-RISK APPETITE

In general, retail companies have medium-risk appetites. The nature of the retail business requires companies in this category to maintain hypervigilance over consumer trends, such as buying habits and tastes, which is all predicated on a lot of guesswork. Therefore, retailers have to make the equivalent of bets every season to determine what kind of products to stock, what colors to choose, where to deliver them, what price to sell them at, and more. The inherent uncertainty of the retail industry and its inevitable reliance on fashion makes it riskier than, say, an insurance company, but less risky than trading stocks.

## HIGH-RISK APPETITE

Brokerage firms are practically the definition of a high-risk company. Of course, stock trading companies have internal and external forces putting limits on the risks they take with investor money, but within those boundaries, there are still many opportunities for risky organizational behavior. The most obvious example is a company that operates within Securities and Exchange Commission (SEC) regulations but still trades in risky investments.

The administrator account on your computer, whether at home or at work, has the permissions required to do anything—not only on that specific device but sometimes on the entire network. By default, when you buy a new computer, you are the administrator. You are allowed to install software or add new hardware. There is nothing an administrator cannot do. In your company, you often use the administrator account to do your daily work, including sending emails, writing documents, and browsing the web.

It's common practice for executives to use their administrator account when doing their everyday business because it puts them in control. If something goes wrong with their computer, they (or, more likely, their IT team) have all the permissions they need to follow troubleshooting steps without having to work around admin permissions.

Makes sense, right? Well, the problem with this common practice is that malicious code writers and phishing attackers *know* that executives use their computers through an administrator account, which makes you an even more likely victim of cyberattacks. Instead, use a nonadmin account when conducting your everyday business activities, such as emailing and browsing the web. It protects both you and your company from an increased risk of a data breach or massive systems failure.

Germs prefer a weakened immune system to breach in order to make you sick. Most computer viruses and malicious codes work in the same way and are worthless without the ability to utilize the kind of omnipotent permissions that come with administrator access. Switching to a less privileged account is easy, and it makes the majority of malicious code inert. It's like wearing gloves while cleaning a public bathroom.

At its most basic level, malicious code goes into your computer to change the files that operate your machine. Ideally, those files should never change. Effective malicious code simply borrows your permissions to infect your computer. If you are running as the administrator and you're attacked by a virus, that malicious code has the master key to everything on your computer. It can go anywhere and do anything it likes.

If you're infected by malicious code and you're not operating as the administrator, the attacker cannot steal the master key from you because you're not carrying it. By running as a less privileged user, you're circumventing your attacker's assumption that all executives naively operate as administrators, which stops the attack before it happens. If the malicious code can't fulfill its instructions, the attacker simply finds another computer to infect the same way a germ that can't get through a healthy immune system will seek out another host.

Using an admin account might make your life easier in the short term—you'll have free rein over your computer—but in the long term, it will leave you and your company's private data susceptible to attack.

## REGULARLY BACK UP YOUR DATA

Ransomware is one of the nastiest types of cyberattacks.

When ransomware infects your computer, its first directive is to encrypt all of your files, meaning your device can no longer read and access them. The criminal behind the virus (which could be an individual or even a North Korean soldier) will then hold your files hostage until you pay for him to unencrypt them.

Regularly backing up your data is your best defense against this kind of attack, because if you have a second copy of all your data on, say, a hard drive, then you won't lose it forever if an attacker compromises your computer. You can wipe your machine clean, reinstall your operating system and programs, and restore your data. Yes, you will lose some time, but your ability to get back in business is entirely under your control.

Modern versions of ransomware can actually detect local backups—even on external hard drives—and it will encrypt all of that data as well. Therefore, because of the sophistication of modern ransomware, it's essential to regularly maintain two different types of backups: your local backup on your computer or an external hard drive, and a second backup that is not directly connected to your computer, such as the cloud.

Your second backup should be located in the cloud, which means the data is not connected to your computer. You may ask, "Why don't I just back up *everything* to the cloud and not even bother with a local backup?" It's a fair question, but there is a good reason to maintain both types of backups.

You never know what type of computer disaster may strike. Yes, you'll always be susceptible to some type of cyberattack, but you could still leave your computer in a taxi cab or airplane and never get it back. In that case, if you have a local backup, you can then buy a new computer, plug in your local hard drive, and restore your data.

But what if you're at work and your house catches fire? What if you go out to dinner and your home is robbed, and the burglars took the local copy of your data? That's why you keep a cloud backup: because you can still restore your data if you lose the physical copy of your backup.

### BACKUP RESTORATION SPEED

One major deterrent for using cloud backups is that the restoration speed is slow. Restoring a backup from the cloud is wholly dependent of the speed of your Internet connection, which, in an average American household, is only 8 MBps (megabytes per second) for download. Compare that to the speed of a USB 3-connected external hard drive, which is 5,120 MBps.

In short, restoring from a local backup is 640 times faster than restoring from a cloud backup.

Having two backups is simply the smart thing to do.

And if something drastic happens, such as your cloud-based data is compromised or your cloud services company goes under, you still have a local copy to restore.

## ENCRYPT YOUR OWN DATA BEFORE ANYONE ELSE CAN

There are two major risks inherent to storing data with a cloud services provider: the company's integrity and the threat of data theft. Anybody can say that they protect your data at all costs, but do they really follow through on that claim? And it's always a possibility that someone could break into your backup with the cloud services company and steal your data.

To neutralize any concerns about the competency of a cloud provider, the threat of theft, and even the possibility of the government taking it under a court-approved warrant, encrypt your data before you upload it to the cloud. If you encrypt it first, no one can make any sense of it, even if they access it.

How do you encrypt your data? First, make sure you use a cloud backup service that gives you complete control over the private encryption key. Most providers won't give you control over your private encryption, and of the few that will, SpiderOak One is the best I've found for personal use.

If you do work with a company that gives you control over the encryption key, store it in two places. Keep one copy in your password manager (see the next section for more details). Then print it on a piece of paper (without your user ID and password on it) and put it wherever you store other vital documents, such as your certified copy of your birth certificate and your passport.

If you are ever burglarized and that paper is stolen, part of your recovery will require you to contact your cloud services provider and follow the process to change the encryption key. If you get struck with terrible luck, and your computer gets stolen at the same time your paper version of the private key is stolen, you will still be able to retrieve your encryption key in your password manager. That's the virtue of having multiple copies of your data.

In my line of work, we call that the "belt and suspenders" approach.

All of the preceding advice for backing up your personal computer applies to your company computers and devices as well. Talk to your IT team about how they execute data backups, where those backups are stored, if they have multiple copies, whether they use encryption, and how they use it.

Once you establish a consistent backup process, make

sure you continue to back up your company's data at regular intervals. An ideal cadence might be between once and three times a day for the best results.

## PASSWORD HYGIENE

There's nothing hygienic about writing down your password on a Post-It Note and slapping it to the side of your computer monitor. But that's how a lot of people save their passwords. Do you and your company a favor and use a high-quality password manager.

One of the big problems with passwords—other than choosing extremely common, guessable passwords—is that people reuse them across platforms and accounts. If you are using very common and reusable passwords, it's easy for a cyberattacker to compromise your account.

This is why banks now send a PIN to your mobile number when you log in. A customer would create an account at Bank of America with a password of 123456, then they would create an account on a much less secured website—

for example, a genealogy website such as MyHeritage, which was compromised in 2018—using the same user ID and password.

Bank security—even online—is very good, so rather than attack the bank, as a cybercriminal, I'll get the consumer's password from the genealogy website, which isn't as secure as the bank. I can steal an entire database of user ID and password combinations from a poorly secured website, then take those combinations, feed them into software designed to exploit them, and then automatically attack the bank's website. The cyberattacker's goal is to find the weakest link in the chain and exploit you, and that weakest link is easier to find if you repeat passwords and user IDs.

By enabling two-step authentication (also called two-factor authentication) with your financial institution, you can prevent someone from accessing your bank account online, even if they have your login and password. If you've ever received a text message with a series of numbers that you have to type into the bank's website, then you've already done this. If not, then look into it.

Turning on two-factor authentication on every website where it's available will go a long way to deterring or preventing someone from stealing your data. Every time you make it even slightly more difficult for a cybercriminal to steal from you, the more likely it is that they'll stop their attack entirely and move on to an easier target.

Moreover, if you use a password manager, you no longer have to remember all of your passwords and PINs, which is one of the main reasons why people reuse them. If you don't have to remember them each time you log in to an account, not only can you choose a unique password for every site, but you can also choose long, complicated passwords—things you could never remember on your own. Even better, your password manager will enter your credentials into the webpage for you. You get better security and it's easier to use. What a great combination!

> Your goal is to use the longest, most complicated password that a website will permit. Ideally, let your password manager generate a random set of characters for your password. Don't use your birth year, your hometown, or anything else that can be found in public records or social media about you.

## PASSWORD RECOVERY: SECURITY QUESTIONS

Similar to easy-to-guess passwords, people often make their security questions easy to guess too. Part of the reason they're easy to guess is because the questions are poorly designed. The questions will include ones such as, "What high school did you go to?" and "What town were you born in?" The problem is that all of that information is public record, not to mention that most people have divulged that information on Facebook at one time or another.

One uncommon strategy to improve your password strength is to set nonobvious answers to your security questions, then store those nonobvious answers in your password manager. If the security question is, "What was your first car?" instead of saying it was a Chevy Nova (which may be true), choose an alpha-numeric response that doesn't fit the prompt, such as Applechicken22. No one is ever going to guess that, and the person to whom you are trying to prove your identity doesn't care what the answer is as long as it matches what they have on file. The reason security questions are generally focused on things you can easily remember is because you never want to forget those answers; otherwise, you can't prove you are who you say you are. Unfortunately, the easier they are to remember, the easier they are for an attacker to guess.

## HOW EASY IT CAN BE

Chris Chaney, the Hollywood hacker who spied on dozens of stars' email accounts for years, used an incredibly basic technique to break into his first victim's email: he guessed their email address by using their first name followed by their last name in Gmail, then reset their password by guessing the answer to the password reset question. For the first celebrity he hacked, the question was, "What is the name of your pet?" the answer to which Chaney found available to the public on the IMDb website. Using this technique, he hacked into and leaked nude pictures of Scarlett Johansson, Christina Aguilera, Renee Olstead, and others.

Use a high-quality password manager to store your passwords as well as your nonobvious answers to security questions. LastPass and 1Password both have a secure note feature built in, which means you can include your security question answers.

One valid criticism of password managers is that if someone hacks into that account, they will have access to everything. My response is simple: if you're going to put all of your eggs into one basket, make sure it's a strong basket.

### TWO-FACTOR AUTHENTICATION

Authentication is based on one of three things: something you know, something you have, or something you are. Let me give you a few examples: something you know is a password. Something you have is a token, such as an app on your smartphone. Something you are is a biometric, such as your fingerprint or the shape of your face.

With all three of these factors, the premise is that it's very hard for someone to impersonate you because they don't know what you know, have what you have, and are not what you are. It is very hard to steal from you in all three of those factors. If you have a great password, hardly anyone will be able to get it. If you're very good about protecting your mobile phone, it will be difficult to steal from you. As long as you don't have the habit of scanning your fingerprints and publishing them on the Internet, it's unlikely that anyone will steal them either.

But protecting you and your company's private data is not as simple as utilizing just one of these authentications. That's why I suggest you use what's called two-factor authentication wherever it's available to you. In short, two-factor authentication means you have to prove you have access to two of the three factors—what you know, what you have, and what you are—in order to access your secured accounts.

> Here is a fantastic resource to help you determine which websites offer two-factor authentication: https://twofactorauth.org.

## TEXT PIN

Not all authentication is created equal. Many banking institutions use a PIN sent via text message to authenticate your login. Many US banks use this authentication technique, mostly because it's easy for customers to use. But this is not a truly secure two-factor authentication technique.

First, if a cybercriminal steals your phone (or even just your phone number), they can intercept your PIN. Second, the mobile phone system that handles text messages has absolutely no security of any kind. It was never designed to do anything that required secrecy. Because of that, cybercriminals have become good at hacking into that system and intercepting text messages.

Let's run through a hypothetical situation to show how this might look in practice. Imagine a cybercriminal steals your mobile phone number and attempts to log in to your bank account. They call T-Mobile from a brand-new mobile phone and tell the representative, "I just bought a new iPhone, so I'd like to move my number from my old phone."

The T-Mobile representative will ask the caller to verify they are the authorized account holder (which, of course, they aren't). More often than not, they'll ask for the last four digits of your Social Security Number, or a security question that has an easy-to-find answer online. Once the cybercriminal "proves" that they're you, the T-Mobile rep will release your phone number from the old phone and assign it to the new iPhone, which deactivates service to your mobile phone. Once that process is complete, the criminal now owns your phone number and can receive every text message sent to it. One by one the criminal will take control of your online accounts by doing password resets along with the actual PIN texted to your phone number.

To keep your mobile phone number from being stolen, set a random account owner PIN with the mobile phone carrier and store it in your password manager.

If you want to move away from PINs via text messages as a second factor of authentication, use a mobile app such as Google Authenticator or Microsoft Authenticator. These apps use one-time passwords that are mathematically generated. Most popular websites are compatible.

## IPHONE SECURITY

Despite the text messaging system itself being insecure, the iPhone is a very secure phone. In fact, even law enforcement struggles to get data from an iPhone, and they don't like that. Apple has a special chip that they designed specifically for security, and the chip is part of a subsystem called the Security Enclave. That is a place where you can store secrets on your iPhone that no one can access, like an uncrackable safe. Just be sure to set at least a six-digit unlock code.

In the early days of mobile phones, up until the iPhone came on the scene, it was very easy for law enforcement to get info from people's phones. They even had dedicated workstations in police stations for downloading information from suspects' and victims' phones. The latest iPhone models do not allow them to do that. It will only give information if the owner authenticates it.

Two-factor authentication is very secure. When it's done well and in combination with a password manager, it's your best option for protecting your sensitive data, for both you and your company. Start with the institutions that carry your most sensitive data—such as banks and cloud services—and enable two-factor authentication if they make it available.

## SOFTWARE UPDATES

In the world we live in today, if I had to choose between having an antivirus package on my computer or having the latest updates installed, I would never use an antivirus package again. That may sound surprising, but the greatest risk to our computing infrastructure today is cyberattacks that operate under the base assumption that you have not installed the latest updates to guard against malicious code.

It's simple. Anytime your software or operating system has an update available, *update it* whether you have a desktop, laptop, tablet, or mobile phone. But if you're like most people, you put it off until your device forces you to update or you get a virus.

Just one month before the NotPetya attack in April 2017, Microsoft released an update that would have stopped the virus from exploiting users' computers. Did everyone utilize this update? Of course not. That's what allowed the virus to spread across Europe and the world.

But the people who did download the update protected their computer and information. This is one of the simplest, most effective cyberhygiene habits you can practice. Had everyone been vigilant about installing updates as soon as they were released, the impact of NotPetya would have been so small that it wouldn't have even been worth noting.

A common reason users do not install updates in a timely manner is because they don't understand the need for it. A new update is released. A user reads the description and says, "Whatever. That doesn't make any sense to me. It's a bunch of security and technical jargon, so it must not be important." They aren't acutely aware of the threats—like NotPetya—that can cause them harm specifically because they didn't install the update. The idea of a software update is very ethereal. You can't see it or feel it, so it makes the need for the update less clear.

**BUGGY SOFTWARE UPDATES: A DIFFERENT FEAR FOR A DIFFERENT TIME**

Unfortunately, you may have grown up in an era when installing a software update was risky. It could either break the system outright, or it greatly reduced the performance of your entire system or a specific application. This happened when updates were not well tested or they were put out so quickly that they had flaws or defects.

This was a much more common occurrence in the past, and while it still happens today, it is much less common, and it's therefore far riskier to ignore updates than it is to install them.

Microsoft understands the importance of software updates, which is why the consumer version of Windows 10 automatically updates. No matter how frustrating it is, you don't have the ability to turn that automatic update feature off.

Commercial-grade versions of Windows, on the other

hand, still allow companies the option to decide which updates to install. That distinction is significant because companies, unlike individuals, lose significant revenues when their systems don't perform sufficiently. As a result of their ability to delay updates, most companies using Windows don't immediately install updates because it could cost them millions of dollars in revenue if they were to go offline due to a wonky update. Therefore, instead of installing immediately, they put the updates through a testing protocol, which might take as long as several weeks.

That's what happened with the EternalBlue exploit. Even though Microsoft published their update in March 2017, a month before NotPetya was released into the wild, most companies hadn't finished testing the update and installing it on their systems, which is why they were so vulnerable. Cybercriminals are recognizing this trend, which is why cycle time between the public release of an update and the release of an exploit is shrinking. It's getting to the point where companies cannot test and install updates fast enough to guard against the damage of a malicious code.

Our digital adversaries are constantly studying and improving, and if you don't do the same, you'll be vulnerable. You can't stand still and expect to survive. That's why I call criminals like Bogachev our new competitors:

because they are constantly learning how to outmaneuver us in their ability to steal our digital assets, the same way a competitor would try to steal our revenues. We must learn to outmaneuver them back. If a new competitor comes into town and starts selling what you're selling but for 30 percent less, what do you do? You have to innovate or go out of business.

If you can adopt that mindset—viewing the adversary on the Internet as you would a competitor that you face in the market—you'll be better prepared and more likely to install updates as they become available.

## EMAIL HYGIENE

Most commonly, email cyberattacks come in the form of phishing attacks. Phishing is a unique digital attack because it preys on the victim's emotions rather than a specific technological manipulation. The best way to guard against phishing attacks is to think more critically about your email messages. Many people think a phishing email will be easy to detect—such as a letter from a Nigerian prince asking for your Social Security Number—but they're becoming much more sophisticated than that.

## SPEAR-PHISHING ATTACKS

As an executive, you should *expect* to be targeted for phishing attempts. You have more assets for cybercriminals to steal, so they'll invest more into hacking you. You won't get one of their mass emails that they send to a million people. The attacker will conduct reconnaissance using social media and other techniques to learn about your work and personal life. That's when they'll send you a spear-phishing attack.

If your twenty-year college reunion is coming up and cybercriminals see it on your LinkedIn profile, they could easily craft a malicious email that says they work with the reunion committee and they'd love you to give the keynote speech. The email could direct you to click a link or download a document, stating it is a predrafted announcement of your giving the keynote. "Why don't you take a look and let me know what you think," the email might say. Feeling flattered by the invitation, you click the link to see the details, but you've also been silently infected with a virus that will log all of your keystrokes and take images of your screen every minute. This data will ultimately be sent back to your attackers.

Instead of sending you a personal email, a spear-phisher might send you an email that looks like it's from your alma mater, asking you to update your alumni username and password. They'll even use the logo and seal of your university to make it look official. If you have a habit of reusing the same ID and password on multiple websites without two-factor authentication, the attackers will soon have their way with your other accounts.

If you are worth the extra effort (maybe you don't fall so easily for the previous spear-phishing attempts), the phisher might send an email purporting to be from Microsoft saying, "We have detected here at Microsoft Central that your computer is infected. We want to help you, so give us a call." If you call them, a very articulate person will answer the phone, confirm the email, then walk you through a procedure designed to remove the malicious code from your computer. Yet the opposite is actually happening. Your computer wasn't infected, but now that you're talking to someone on the phone, they get you to grant them permission to remotely become the administrator for your computer. Then, under the guise of helping you, they install malicious code.

## HOW TO PROTECT YOURSELF AGAINST PHISHING ATTACKS

If all levels of phishing attacks are becoming harder and harder to detect, then how can you as a busy executive protect yourself? My first suggestion is to visit opendns.com/phishing-quiz to test your readiness for a cyberattack.

Your next step, as an executive, is to go through a specific set of actions whenever you receive unexpected email attachments or links. The first thing to do is back away from the keyboard, take a deep breath, and ask yourself, "Does this relate to a matter I'm already involved in?" This helps you assess the message for authenticity. If the answer is no, you should be extremely cautious about whether the email is real.

If the email appears to come from someone you know, but it isn't about something you are actively working on, either call that person or create a new email to ask, "Hey, I just got this from you. Tell me about it. Is this something new? Did you send it?" Again, it's very important that you don't just click Reply to ask the sender "Is this legitimate?" because if it is a phisher, they'll reply, "Of course it is!"

They are counting on you trying to resolve this matter so quickly that you just hit the Reply button instead of creating a new email.

---

**WHAT MAKES US SUSCEPTIBLE TO ATTACKS?**

I firmly believe that many accounts payable clerks and administrators fall for attacks asking them to move money to offshore bank accounts because they are so in the flow of getting their work done that they don't take the time to pause and ask, "Is this for real?" The same thing happens with executives. You must interrupt that cycle of wanting to be highly productive. If you don't interrupt that cycle, the momentum of your day will eventually cause you to open a dangerous email and follow the phisher's instructions.

---

## HOW TO STEAL A HOUSE

Wire fraud—where phishers get people to move money to their account—is becoming much more prevalent today, especially in real estate transactions. In one case, a couple in the process of purchasing a house was taken advantage of by a phisher. They received instructions via email from what they thought was their escrow officer, asking them to wire $500,000. They later went into the mortgage brokerage and discovered that the money had not been received. The email they'd acted on was from a cybercriminal.

The couple was only able to recoup half of their money, but that is still an incredibly large sum to lose. What can you do to make sure you're not the victim of such an attack? When you receive wire instructions by email, never use that email or any of the information in it to verify the instructions.

Look up the person's contact information yourself, then use that to contact the person and verify the wiring instructions. Approach every situation that involves the transfer of large sums of money with a healthy amount of suspicion. The Internet was never designed to be secure and to protect confidential banking information. It was designed by the military to survive a nuclear attack. We aren't using it for its originally intended purpose, so you have to be the last defense for yourself.

You may feel you don't have the time to stop and make a phone call or send a new email anytime you receive something that might be suspicious. In response, I'd like to remind you that most people are not adept at recognizing phishing emails. Even if you're confident you're not at risk of receiving malicious code, that doesn't change the fact that you're going to be targeted. It's just a matter of time, and there are armies of cybercriminals working down the list of names. The time it takes to verify suspicious emails is miniscule compared to the time and efficiency a successful phishing attack will take from you and your company.

## ADVANCED HANDWASHING TECHNIQUES

Recognizing and avoiding phishing attacks will help you prevent a large portion of computer viruses and malicious codes. There are still several advanced techniques and tools you can use to help you keep away destructive digital germs.

### AD BLOCKING

Did you know that advertisements shown on a webpage you visit are usually served up from a dedicated ad network? Not only do those ads slow down your web browser, but they are also a popular means of delivering malicious code to your computer. That's why ad blockers exist. Ad-blocking software does exactly what it sounds like: it blocks ads from appearing on your web browser.

When you pull up a news story on Forbes.com, you are accessing Forbes's web server and viewing a piece of content—such as an article or video—that they are storing and have complete control over. If that page has an ad, it's coming from a different company, meaning Forbes has no control over it. A company like Forbes will have great cybersecurity, but the companies that display ads are notorious for having terrible security. Attackers know that, so they'll focus on exploiting you through their advertisements rather than the website itself. In fact, for two weeks in summer 2016 that's exactly what happened: the Forbes website was compromised via ad servers. Simply visiting the site without an ad blocker made visitors vulnerable to a malicious code attack.

Which ad blockers are best for protecting yourself from ad-based attacks?

You can choose specific web browsers with built-in ad blockers, or you can download software that blocks ads. If you want to stick with your current web browser, I recommend uBlock Origin. If you want to switch to a new browser, Brave—which was released in 2016—is your best choice.

> One very popular ad blocker that I would not recommend is Ad Block Plus. Ad Block Plus was built in response to the opinion that advertisements are annoying but not dangerous. As a result, Ad Block Plus allows advertisers to pay them a fee to still show their ads. Their entire promise is antithetical to ad-blocking cybersecurity.

## ONLY USE APPS DOWNLOADED DIRECTLY FROM APPLE OR GOOGLE

An attacker can hide malicious code in a software download. If you install an app from a third-party website—not the iTunes Store or Google Play store—that app isn't subject to the same testing process. Apple and Google heavily scrutinize apps and only put them in their catalogs once they're convinced they do not pose a threat. It isn't entirely foolproof—a few malicious apps do get through here and there—but when that happens, though, the mistake is discovered quickly, and Apple or Google then notify you immediately so you can delete it.

There are many third-party software download sites for Android, such as Handango, Android Games Room, and MoboMarket. They often attract people away from the Google Play store by boasting faster download speeds, powerful servers, and an ever-changing library of software available. But those third-party software download websites don't have the same cybersecurity processes to detect bad apps that Google does, so they are generally more likely to serve you an app with malicious code, which can steal your browsing history, your keystrokes, and other sensitive data.

## TURN ON WINDOWS DEFENDER

Most people don't realize this, but Windows comes with its own antivirus software called Windows Defender (previously called Microsoft Security Essentials). You just have to make sure it's turned on to utilize it. Most people are still in the habit of buying third-party antivirus packages such as Norton or McAfee, but those programs cost more, tend to slow your computer down, and are not as effective as the built-in Windows Defender program.

## FREEZE YOUR CREDIT ACCOUNTS

Cybercriminals are always developing new ways to exploit users, but if you follow all of the handwashing techniques I've outlined in this chapter, your chances of being infiltrated by a virus will go down significantly for both you and your company.

It is still possible that despite all of your precautions, you can have your identity stolen. Cybercriminals love to steal identities because it is much more lucrative than stealing just your credit card. Card issuers have a sophisticated fraud detection system, and will quickly shut off a card or notify you, the card holder, if they detect suspicious activity. However, if I steal your identity, I can open up multiple lines of credit, even beyond credit cards. I can even file fraudulent medical claims in your name, which also reduces the amount of insurance coverage available to you.

### WHAT EXACTLY IS IDENTITY THEFT?

The best definition of identity theft is this: when someone obtains sufficient personal information about you to open lines of credit in your name or borrow on your existing credit. The ways in which people can use your identity are surprising. Some people have had their homes refinanced or sold without realizing it until they get a bank statement or other notification after the fact.

The best defense against identity theft is freezing your credit files at every major credit bureau. Freezing your credit file means nobody can open a new line of credit in your name—including you. Upon freezing, each credit bureau will give a personal ID number you can use to unfreeze your credit file when, at some point in the future, you want to get a mortgage or buy a car. Then, after you open the new line of credit, you can refreeze your credit lines. This is burdensome process, and I recognize that, but it is the best preventive measure you can take to protecting your identity. If your identity is stolen and someone tries to open a line of credit in your name, they will simply be blocked from doing so.

## WHITELISTING: A VERY ADVANCED HANDWASHING TECHNIQUE

If you are serious about cyberhygiene and you have the technical skills (or know someone who does), then you can get a lot of protection against malicious code by turning on application whitelisting.

Application whitelisting prevents unapproved and malicious programs and installers from running on your computer regardless of whether the software was downloaded from a website, clicked on as an email attachment, or introduced via CD/DVD/USB removable storage media.

Implementing application whitelisting on servers can help prevent adversaries from running malware that steals your passwords or otherwise provides them with additional privileges.

Microsoft has had built-in support for application whitelisting since Windows 7 using a feature called AppLocker. It can be configured on a single computer or deployed centrally by your IT department.

Again, this is very advanced compared to the other cyberhygiene practices we've reviewed, but when set up properly, it works. Unfortunately, you need one of the more expensive versions of Windows to use it.

## HANDWASHING: NOT EXCITING BUT NECESSARY

I don't know of anyone who wakes up in the morning looking forward to how much they'll get to wash their hands throughout the day. Nobody looks forward to getting a flu shot or getting their blood pressure checked. But you take those preventive measures so you don't get sick. You need to make the same choices with respect to your cyberhealth. Cybergerms are everywhere, and the only way to keep them from infecting your and your company's sensitive data is by implementing good cyberhygiene on a regular basis.

Start by implementing the most impactful cyberhygiene techniques—such as limiting admin account usage and performing regular data backups—that I front-loaded in this chapter. Then, as you get a system in place for each hygienic practice, move down the priority list to include handwashing techniques such as whitelisting applications, utilizing Windows Defender, and freezing your credit files.

A large percentage of data breaches are the result of insiders making mistakes. By practicing all of the handwashing techniques I've detailed in this chapter, you and your company will be further on the journey to reasonable cybersecurity at home and in the office.

What if you travel for work? Many busy executives have extensive travel schedules, which add unique challenges to cyberhygiene.

How do you maintain your cyberhealth while you're traveling for work?

# CYBERHYGIENE AND WORK TRAVEL

I walked off the stage at my local Rotary Club, having just finished a presentation called "Ten Steps to Mastering Cybersecurity for Home and Business." A retired schoolteacher named Hank, likely in his early seventies, approached me to tell me his cybersecurity story: he had nearly lost his entire life savings while on a recent vacation.

While he was out of town, somebody called Hank's broker claiming to be Hank and requested that all of the funds in his brokerage account—the entirety of his modest life savings—be transferred to a new financial institution. The phisher (yes, they use the phone as well as email) claiming to be the schoolteacher had all of the information necessary to prove his false identity: the last four digits of Hank's social security number, answers to common security questions, and date of birth. All information readily available online if one had an incentive to look.

This phisher had an incentive.

Luckily for Hank, his broker knew him and his voice personally, so when the phisher called the brokerage to fraudulently transfer his life savings, the broker knew it was not Hank's voice. Moreover, the broker knew that Hank was out of the country, so the broker stopped the phishing attack.

After Hank told me this story, I had to ask, "Do you think it was a coincidence that somebody made this attack while you were on vacation?"

"Sure it was," he said.

"I hate to say it, Hank, but this was absolutely *not* a coincidence. This attack was designed specifically to exploit you while you were on vacation."

He was incredulous. "How could anybody have known I was gone?"

It turned out that, like most people, Hank had posted

about his trip on social media, making him an easy target for an attack. Hank was incredibly lucky that his broker knew him well enough to recognize his voice and know that he was out of the country. Likewise, if Hank were an executive with multiple millions of dollars in his account, the attack might have been more sophisticated.

As we learned about Austria-based aerospace company FACC in the introduction, the business email compromise attack—one in which phishers seek out a big payday by targeting one specific person in a large organization—would involve more intense preparation and execution. The attack would likely revolve around your email: the phishers would silently compromise your email, continue to monitor it, and wait for the perfect opportunity to throw the harpoon into the water—during one of your trips.

They could potentially learn exactly when you'll be gone, which hotel you're staying at, what airline you're flying, and maybe even your seat number. Then, when you go out of town, they make their move.

Even if you never post about it on Facebook.

Just like Hank, you and your company become more vulnerable to a cyberattack while you're on vacation or a business trip. Not only are phishers more likely to strike when you're not in the office, but you also become more lax with your cyberhygiene when you're traveling for work.

You go on work trips and personal vacations specifically to do things you can't do at home. When you travel—especially for work—you're on a mission, and that mission rarely includes proper cyberhygiene. The psychological distance you feel from your work while you travel—along with your very real geographical distance—make for a perfect environment for your cybersecurity to be compromised.

In this chapter, I'll teach you some of the surprising cybersecurity risks you face while traveling, and I'll give you specific measures you can take to ensure that you protect yourself and your company's sensitive data when you're away from home.

### CYBERCRIMINALS ARE AMORAL

Like germs, cybercriminals do not care if you're a good person, if you're a child, or if you're a charitable organization. They will attack pediatric dentists, charitable organizations, and retired schoolteachers just as soon as they target government and corporate entities. A target is a target to them. They just want money or data that can be easily turned into money.

## STOLEN DATA AT THE BORDER

The war on terrorism has reached a fever pitch. The use of social media for distributing terrorist propaganda is so effective that the United States now wants access to the social media accounts of people entering our country. As a result, the federal government now closely inspects mobile devices, such as laptops and mobile phones, that people carry on their person when they cross the border into our country. No "reasonable suspicion" is required inside the border zone.

How can they do this?

Because the border is not considered part of the interior of the United States, they claim it is a unique space with special laws and regulations. Therefore, border guards have increased abilities to search at the border—abilities that a police officer on Main Street wouldn't have. *Within* our country's borders, we still have constitutional protections against unreasonable search and seizure—as protected by the Fourth Amendment—but those protections don't fully exist in the border zone.

Even in places far removed from the border, deep into the interior of the country, immigration officials enjoy broad—though not limitless—powers. Specifically, federal regulations give US Customs and Border Protection (CBP) the authority to operate within one hundred miles of any US "external boundary." In this one-hundred-mile zone, Border Patrol agents have certain additional authorities. For instance, Border Patrol can operate immigration checkpoints.

Granted, they cannot pull anyone over without "reasonable suspicion" of an immigration violation or crime, nor can they search vehicles in the one-hundred-mile zone without a warrant or "probable cause." Yet they often do conduct warrantless searches in the one-hundred-mile zone the same way they conduct searches at the border crossing itself.

What does this mean for you as a traveling executive?

Be careful if you encounter Border Patrol in the one-hundred-mile border zone. They do not have the same authority to conduct suspicionless searches of travelers' electronic devices as they do at the ports of entry. They have rules, but they don't always follow them because they expect you as the traveler to let them do whatever they want, including searching and copying your electronic devices.

For perspective: this border zone includes downtown Seattle, Chicago, Boston, New York City, Miami, San Antonio, Phoenix, Los Angeles, and San Francisco.

Roughly two-thirds of the United States' population (200 million people) live within the one hundred-mile zone, that is, within one hundred miles of a US land or coastal border.

See the risk to your digital data?

If you fail to comply with their commands to unlock your devices at a port of entry, you can even be refused entry to the United States if you aren't a citizen. If you are a citizen, they can detain you for hours at a time. If they do gain access to your device -whether it's with your permission or without it—they can and will make a full copy of all of your data and retain it, even after they release you.

I don't say all of this to scare you. Like everything else in this book, I'm only informing you so you can better protect your digital assets. If your work travel brings you across the US border, expect to be asked to unlock your device for a border inspection. If you carry sensitive data for your personal accounts, your company accounts, or your clients—such as passwords, trade secrets, or payroll information—you may violate the confidentiality of that data. Even though you're not a terrorist or a threat to national security, if you let border agents copy your devices, you have no idea what happens to it after that.

So what should you do to stop these potential border breaches of your sensitive data? I'll use myself as an example. In my line of work, I must be incredibly careful about the data I carry on my devices. Not only do I have all of my secrets on my devices, but I also know all of the cyberdetails of my customers.

I traveled to Italy recently and took an iPhone and iPad with me to do work on the trip. Before I left home, I reset both devices to their factory defaults, meaning I wiped them of all sensitive data for myself and my customers. That way, if border agents remotely copied my device at the airport or at the border, the most they would get was a few travel apps and my travel itinerary rather than a host of account passwords and other sensitive information. Then, once I landed in my destination, I accessed all of the necessary data for work from my cloud services.

Even if you don't take measures as extreme as I do when you travel for work, at the very least, understand the possibility that border agents—for the United States and many other countries—may try to copy your data when you cross an international border. Ask yourself if there's anything on your phone or tablet you wouldn't want in the hands of someone else. If there is, then it's best to delete that data or store it with a cloud service until your international travel is complete.

For a more detailed guide on how to protect your digital privacy at the border, visit this page on the Electronic Frontier Foundation website: http://b.link/border.

## REQUIRE DUAL SIGNATURES FOR LARGE TRANSACTIONS

According to the FBI, since 2013, email compromises have cost companies across the globe more than $12.5 billion. The vast majority of those compromises would not have happened had there been a stronger set of authorizations to approve the movement of money.

Let's say you're on a work trip, and while you're out of town, an accounts payable clerk receives an email purporting to be from you saying, "Please transfer $2 million to our client's account. I'm on a business trip right now, so please take care of it. Thank you." If this happened at your company, would the accounts payable clerk have the authority to make that transaction?

If the answer is yes, you should reassess your system for authorizing large transactions. You should have a policy requiring every authorized employee to seek out another approver, confirming that the transaction request is authentic. This is called dual-signature authorization. By utilizing this system, the odds that your company will be compromised on account of your absence will go down significantly.

Like most good cyberhygiene practices, requiring a dual signature costs very little time and almost no money. You just have to commit yourself and your employees to doing it regularly.

---

### NOT JUST AN IT PROBLEM

Whether you're at home or abroad, your technology team is not your only defense against fraud. You should train everyone—especially people who have the authority to move money—to resist phishing attacks. As I've said, phishing is an attack on a person's emotions, not an attack on technology. Make sure that everyone in your company is emotionally prepared to resist phishing attempts on your company while you're out of town.

---

## AVOID PUBLIC WI-FI

Public Wi-Fi is the equivalent of a swimming pool with an inadequate amount of chlorine: it's likely germ-ridden, full of fecal matter, and everything else that you don't want anywhere near you or your personal property. And just like a public pool, how can you tell immediately whether the water is pristine or filthy? There's no easy way.

Granted, public Wi-Fi is extremely convenient to use, especially during work travel. Unfortunately, it's so convenient that attackers love to hang out there and conduct watering hole attacks.

What is a watering hole attack?

Imagine a watering hole on the plains of Africa. The water is so rare and refreshing that animals of all kinds—including predators and prey—all come together to get a drink. With all of those animals in one confined space together, the antelopes and water buffaloes find themselves face-to-face with constant danger. There's an alligator lurking in the water. There's a cheetah hiding in the brush. A lion sits at the edge of the oasis. Why should they run around chasing prey when they know their next meal will come to them for a drink of water sooner or later?

Now, instead of a watering hole on the plains, think of a public Wi-Fi connection, and you have a better idea of what a watering hole attack entails: you are the prey, and the predators are just waiting for you to come to them. But can you see them before you put your mouth down to the water?

The attacker might use the public Wi-Fi network to send you a dialog box, prompting you to update your Flash player. Although I would normally suggest you update your software as quickly as possible, if you're connected to public Wi-Fi, then it may be a watering hole attack, either by a predator sitting across from you in the coffee shop or someone lying in wait at the website you just pulled up. Wait until you're back on your own home or corporate network—one that is managed by someone you trust to keep it clean—then open a new tab in your browser and search for the legitimate publisher of that software and get the update straight from their website.

Even if you're not actively signed in to a sensitive account—such as your bank or credit card—you're still susceptible to an attack just by being connected to public Wi-Fi. You might say, "Well, when I'm on public Wi-Fi, I only mess around on Facebook or watch TV shows. I don't do anything serious like banking, so I'm secure." That's a flawed and dangerous line of thinking.

The problem is that a watering hole attack might not take place at the actual watering hole. The predator may follow you back home in the form of a malicious code they put on your computer while you were connected to public Wi-Fi. Then, when you're connected to a secure network back home, you'll log in to your bank account, and that malicious code will signal to the criminal that you're ready to be attacked. The lion will follow you home from the watering hole and wait until your guard is down to make its move.

This kind of cyberattack happens at seemingly trustworthy public Wi-Fi hotspots such as libraries, government buildings, and even password-protected private business hotspots. (If you have the password, then I have the password, and everyone at the coffee shop has the password, meaning the network isn't secure.)

Instead of using public Wi-Fi when you travel, utilize your mobile phone's hotspot feature. It may be more expensive in the short term to buy a data plan for a mobile hotspot, but in the long run it will save you more time and money than opening yourself up to the myriad risks of public Wi-Fi.

## USE A VIRTUAL PRIVATE NETWORK

When you connect to a typical computer network, even on your secured home network, the data you send between you and the website you're visiting is observable by other people on your network who are curious and have the right tools. (Most are freely available on the Internet, of course.) Even if you turn on advanced tools that encrypt web traffic, someone might not know what exact data you're sending, but they could still see when you're visiting your bank's website, for example, or your email account. If you use what's called a virtual private network (VPN), it encrypts everything. Nobody can see the data you're sending nor can they see the websites you visit. It's like an invisibility cloak for all of your online activity.

Using a VPN is useful anywhere, but it's especially important while you're traveling. Depending on the country you're traveling to and the profile of your company, you never know when or why a foreign government will monitor you. Protect yourself and your company's assets by using a VPN while you travel for work.

How exactly do you use a VPN?

If your company doesn't already provide a VPN service, you can buy one on the open market. You must be careful, though. Just like password managers, VPNs can range from extremely secure to terrible. (A bad VPN is actually worse than having no VPN at all, since it will only give you the false sense of security without actually providing any protection.) Many people choose free VPNs because, well, they're free. Don't fall into that trap. VPN providers need to make money somehow, so if they offer their service for free, they most often make their money by selling your browser history. In other words, they collect information about all the websites you visit and sell that information to marketers. There goes your privacy. Instead, choose a VPN provider that has engineered their product to be secure and resistant to attack, whether at home or abroad.

## CLOUD COMPUTING ON THE ROAD

The security of cloud computing is predicated on what's called a shared responsibility model. This means that cloud providers offer some security capabilities, but you are expected to take reasonable measures to protect your own data beyond the services they provide. If you use cloud services to access sensitive work data while you travel, which is preferable to keeping that data on your devices, then this shared security model is significant for you.

Let's say you subscribe to Office 365 and you use Word Online. As part of the software as a service (SaaS) product you are buying for $99 per year, Microsoft provides:

- Servers
- Data storage
- Firewalls
- Network security monitoring

- Data backups
- Redundant servers and networks
- Antimalware scanning
- User authentication

This is a great deal, as long as it all works when you really need it.

Now, here's what you need to do yourself in order to keep your end of the secure data bargain:

- Create a strong password that's not shared with anyone else
- Enable a second factor of authentication
- Set the correct permissions so you share your documents only with people who are authorized to see and change them
- Add data-sensitivity labels in the footer of your documents so readers know how to protect them

A cloud service is only as secure as you make it, and if you travel for work, you should make it as secure as possible by turning on and configuring all the security options you need to protect your data.

## DELETE, BURN, REPEAT

If you go overseas and use public Wi-Fi (which, of course, is a terrible idea, but we all make mistakes), there is a good chance you will bring home a malicious code on your device.

This is why it's a good idea to reset your devices when you're done traveling: if they have malicious code on them, that code will be deleted when you reset it to its original factory settings. In the future, expect the attackers to find ways to keep their malicious code on your device even if you completely wipe it.

Ideally, you should use what are called burner devices, meaning you have a blank laptop, cell phone, and tablet that are all completely free of any data. You only use these devices to connect to your cloud services and never keep any sensitive data on them. Then, if these devices are compromised at a border or elsewhere, you can "burn" them without any significant loss besides the cost of the devices themselves.

As an executive, your cybersecurity risks are greater while you travel than they are at home. You not only have to protect yourself against cybercriminals as usual, but you also have to protect yourself from government entities, especially as you cross international borders. There's no such thing as perfect prevention when it comes to cybersecurity, but you can take the measures in the previous two chapters to better protect yourself, whether you're at home or abroad.

# PART TWO

# YOUR CYBER RISK MANAGEMENT GAME PLAN

Up until this point in the book, I've given you tips, advice, and examples for how to practice better personal cyberhygiene at home, at work, and on the road. Now, as we move into part 2, I am giving you the instructions for making a cyber risk management game plan to help your company practice reasonable cybersecurity.

As we've seen, cyberthreats have never been greater, and they will continue to increase for years to come. By releasing the NIST Cybersecurity Framework (see chapter 2), the US government acknowledged this new normal. Putting the majority of our resources into prevention isn't a viable strategy anymore. Instead, we need to practice reasonable cybersecurity.

That phrase—reasonable cybersecurity—is extremely important. It's the new standard for organizations when dealing with cyber risks. As an executive, you must become familiar with what it means and then follow it, because you have some serious forces bearing down on you.

On one side, the adversaries are relentlessly cyberattacking you, and it's only a matter of time before you get breached. So while you work every day to prevent a breach, you also need to prepare yourself to deal with one when it happens with no advance warning. Your public reputation depends on it.

On the other side, the Federal Trade Commission (FTC) says an organization must practice "reasonable security measures" as compared to an entity of similar size and sophistication given the type, amount, and methods of data collected. Do otherwise, and the FTC may charge you with unfair or deceptive acts. Typical FTC consequences for unreasonable cybersecurity include:

- Orders to correct illegal practices
- Twenty years of close oversight of the cybersecurity program

- $40,000 in fines for each new violation

Let me be clear: what follows is a lite version of a product that my customers pay for. This is not just an academic idea of what *could* help your company, or a hypothetical of how you *might* improve your cybersecurity; this is a proven system that works. Although the following system doesn't include all of the features and functionality of the paid program I provide my customers, for most of you, this lite version will be enough to get you into the practice of reasonable cybersecurity.

If you practice every piece of advice that I gave you in part 1 of this book, your cybersecurity will be ahead of 95 percent of executives. But the world has changed. It's not enough for you to practice good cyberhygiene; you need *proof* that your company is practicing reasonable cybersecurity. There's an old management saying that goes, "If you don't write it down, it never happened." Most companies' cybersecurity plans are so disorganized, old, and incomplete that they don't make any sense to outsiders (if they even have a cybersecurity plan). But what happens if someone wants to buy your company, or you find yourself under investigation for a cybersecurity breach? How will you show your reasonable cybersecurity practices without proper implementation *and* documentation?

You also need to shift the culture of your organization

toward good, daily cyberhygiene and the practice of reasonable cybersecurity. Our approach in part 2 uses a high level of engagement with your team to help you make that shift. Not only will you find out what's really going on at the front lines, but you will also be able to use that information to make the changes that will help you thrive in the face of evolving cyber risks. According to John P. Kotter, professor of leadership at the Harvard Business School and *New York Times* best-selling author, producing useful change is at the heart of leadership.

You hold in your hands a practical guide that will help you implement and document your cybersecurity plan so thoroughly that it will not only protect you against reasonable threats, but it will also protect you in the case of potential acquisition and investigation.

What I'm about to share with you is essentially the secret sauce of my company, Cyber Risk Opportunities. It's so important to my company's success that I deeply questioned whether to include it in the book. But because my goal is to teach you, I am including it here. This cyber risk management program will not only exponentially improve your company's cybersecurity, but it will also improve your bottom line and save you enormous amounts of time.

And to make it even easier, we've created and released

an online Cyber Risk Workbook that will help automate your work. When you're ready, go to this URL to access it: http://b.link/cyber-risk-workbook.

# PHASE 1

## DISCOVER YOUR TOP CYBER RISKS

In 2013, a cybercriminal broke into Yahoo's servers and stole their entire database of user IDs and passwords. At the time, Yahoo had close to a billion users, and it took them months to detect the breach.

Yahoo's response to the breach? They buried the story. Yahoo didn't reset those users' passwords, and they didn't notify anyone of what had happened. They simply sat on the information and hoped for the best. In fact, not only was the public kept in the dark, but they also didn't even tell their chief information security officer (CISO). It was about the worst example of cybersecurity incident response I've ever heard of.

Then Yahoo experienced another data breach, at which point they weren't able to keep the first one under wraps anymore. At that point, their CISO caught wind of the initial breach from 2013, and in part because he was deliberately kept in the dark by executive management, he promptly resigned and went to work for Facebook.

Although their entire executive team now knew about both breaches, the general public—including their users and other companies—didn't fully understand the magnitude of the compromise. That's when Verizon came in to make an acquisition offer to the tune of $4.8 billion.

Verizon did their due diligence, and in the process, they discovered the enormity of the data breaches. They also unearthed the full extent of the subsequent cover-ups by the executive team. Verizon used this information to their advantage. Rather than shying away from the deal, they saw the value of the underlying company but knew they could get a major discount on account of Yahoo's cybersecurity negligence. In the end, Verizon bought Yahoo for a $350 million discount.

Yahoo didn't practice reasonable cybersecurity—and if they did, it wasn't implemented correctly, which is just as bad—and Verizon took advantage of their oversight. You can be like Verizon, or you can be like Yahoo, or you can be better than both of them. The choice is yours, and that choice begins by implementing the following three-phase cyber risk management game plan.

When your game plan is in place, you can answer these five questions with confidence:

1. What are the top five cyber risks to my business?
2. Am I getting the biggest return possible for my cyber risk management dollars?
3. Do all of my executives understand our cybersecurity plans?
4. Does everyone at work know how they help mitigate our top cyber risks?
5. What do I tell our biggest customer when they ask, "What are you guys doing about cybersecurity?"

## ATTORNEY-CLIENT PRIVILEGE

I don't expect you to actively manage every cyber risk facing your company. In fact, if you do nothing more than work through the questionnaires on the following pages and identify your risks, you will be ahead of most other executives.

But before you even get started on those questionnaires, I want you to know about attorney-client privilege (ACP) as a way to protect yourself in case your cyber risks manifest themselves differently than you expected.

If one of your cyber risks ends up being the source of a data breach in the future and you didn't prioritize that risk in your cyber risk management game plan, you could be accused of knowing that risk existed but never taking action. This could lead to a charge of negligence in a court of law (to say nothing of the court of public opinion). By conducting this work under attorney-client privilege, you remain in control of your cyber risk records in the face of a request to submit them as evidence.

The disadvantage of creating ACP over your cyber risk management records is that it's more expensive and that it takes longer to get the work done. I'm not an attorney, and this is not legal advice, but here's how you get started: hire an outside attorney with some cyber-security expertise and ask them to contract with a qualified cyber risk expert to perform the work detailed in part 2 of this book. Make sure everyone handles and shares the cyber risk information as instructed by the attorney. We work this way in my company regularly and it's not a problem once the arrangements are put into place.

## THE THREE PHASES OF YOUR CYBER RISK MANAGEMENT GAME PLAN

### PHASE 1: DISCOVER YOUR TOP CYBER RISKS

Phase 1, which takes place over the course of thirty days, is comprised of measuring and scoring your company's current cyber risks. As an executive, you encounter unlimited risks to your company, but your resources to manage those risks are limited, so you need a strict method of prioritization. That's what you'll develop in phase 1: priority.

### PHASE 2: MAKE YOUR CYBER RISK MANAGEMENT GAME PLAN

Phase 2 also takes thirty days, and it results in the creation of your personalized cyber risk management game plan. The game plan you develop will be specifically designed to address your top five cyber risks, which you identified in phase 1.

During phase 2, you will ensure that every dollar you spend on cyber risk management is giving you the greatest value on one of your top five risks as an organization. Your game plan will account for four specific dimensions of business value— technical risk mitigation, increased reliability of operations, legal risk mitigation, and financial returns—to ensure that your game plan is optimized for your company's unique needs. As we've discussed at length in this book, reasonable cybersecurity doesn't mean you completely eliminate your cyber risks; it means you smartly manage those risks while improving your competitive advantage.

## PHASE 3: MAINTENANCE AND UPDATES

Phase 3 lasts ten months, bringing the duration of the entire three-phase plan to a year. Reasonable cybersecurity is a journey. If you identify your top cyber risks and you develop a risk management game plan, that's good, but it's not good enough. You have to actually implement your plan and continue to improve on it. That's what phase 3 is.

In the ten months remaining in your one-year program, you will check in on your organization's handwashing every month and do more in-depth check-ins every quarter. If you notice that part of your company isn't implementing the game plan effectively, this maintenance phase is your opportunity to discover why and come up with a plan to get back on track. It also provides an opportunity to celebrate your company's successes.

## WHAT ABOUT MONTH THIRTEEN?

You'll notice that phase 3 ends one full year after you start phase 1. Does that mean you're done? What happens next? You go back to phase 1 and repeat the three phases. Every year.

You don't have to throw out everything you've done in the first year. On the contrary, you probably already have more cyber risk management work to do based on the cyber risk management game plan you created. To stop now would be wrong. But cyber risks do change as the adversary innovates. Your business changes over time too. Plus, through the interview process, your people will be reminded of the importance of practicing good cyberhygiene and reasonable cybersecurity. So it's wise to repeat this structured, systematic, and comprehensive process every year.

Use the results of phase 1 from year two to refresh your top five cyber risks along with your prioritized cyber risk management game plan.

## PHASE 1, STEP 1: WIDEN YOUR SCOPE

Before you set the foundation of your cyber risk management game plan, you almost certainly need to widen the scope of what you want to measure and score. When I go through this process with my customers, most of them are entirely focused on one specific facet of cybersecurity (typically how their technological defenses can be better) and want to focus all of their efforts there. Maybe they think they only need to protect their customers' credit card information, or maybe they want to ensure their users' password data doesn't get leaked. Regardless of the details, I always encourage my customers to widen their scope and to measure every facet of their cybersecurity:

- People, process, management, and technology
- All digital assets, including customer data, payroll data, and trade secrets
- Across all departments in the company

Be sure to include all twenty-three activities in the NIST Cybersecurity Framework. This is not an external audit you're conducting, and you're not subject to a regulator asking for details. This is your choice, and if you're making the choice to improve your cybersecurity, you might as well go all in. If you or your employees hide information, you will only hurt yourselves.

# LISTED BELOW ARE THE TWENTY-THREE ACTIVITIES FROM THE NIST CYBERSECURITY FRAMEWORK

Activities in the Identify function:

1. Asset management
2. Business environment
3. Governance
4. Risk assessment
5. Risk management strategy
6. Supply chain risk management

Activities in the Protect function:

7. Identity management, authentication, and access control
8. Awareness and training
9. Data security
10. Information protection processes and procedures
11. Maintenance
12. Protective technology

Activities in the Detect function:

13. Anomalies and events
14. Security continuous monitoring
15. Detection processes

Activities in the Respond function:

16. Response planning
17. Response communications
18. Response analysis
19. Mitigation
20. Response improvements

Activities in the Recover function:

21. Recovery planning
22. Recovery improvements
23. Recovery communications

**PHASE 1, STEP 2: GET BUY-IN**

This cyber risk management game plan will not work without buy-in from your employees. Getting buy-in starts with the tone you approach people with. You will be passing out a lot of questionnaires, asking people to be open and forthright about their perceptions and activities in your company. In order to get honest responses, you have to approach this from a collaborative mindset. That starts with how you talk about your game plan.

### CONDUCT AN ASSESSMENT, NOT AN AUDIT

Some people use the terms "audit" and "assessment" synonymously, but I don't. To me, they're strikingly dissimilar. An audit is when an outsider evaluates what you're doing, with the expressed interest of finding something you're doing wrong. Audits generally put people on the defensive. Assessments are different. Assessments are management actions designed to identify opportunities for improvement. They're internal, not external. Even if an outsider (such as me) helps, an assessment is owned by management, is internally focused, and is going to a different place than an audit.

Make sure that your team knows that you're not conducting a witch hunt. You will simply be asking questions in order to gather information. To that end, you should be open about the process your company is undertaking, and your email communication should reflect that open, collaborative spirit.

---

**SAMPLE EMAIL TEMPLATE**

To: All Hands

From: CEO

Re: Cyber Risk Assessment

Hello team,

I am extremely concerned about our cybersecurity, and I hope you are too. The crooks are out there, and we can't even begin to imagine the various ways they are penetrating companies and stealing trade secrets, money, customer lists, and generally disrupting businesses.

In order to combat this, we are implementing a cyber risk management plan. Our first step to implementing that plan is to conduct interviews with many of you so we can fully assess our current cyber risks.

The goal of these interviews is to learn how we can best balance our cybersecurity needs with our day-to-day business needs. Each interview will take 30–90 minutes and will be conducted in person here in [city].

[Point of contact name] will be coordinating with each of you to find a workable time slot for your interview.

If you have any questions about the program itself, let me know. If you have questions about the logistics of the interviews, let [point of contact name] know.

Thank you!

[Your name]

---

You will inevitably get questions in return, many of which will spawn from people's anxieties about being interviewed. Be sure that your response to those questions reinforces the collaborative nature of the interviews.

## PHASE 1, STEP 3: SELECT INTERVIEWEES

As a general rule of thumb, if your company has approximately $100 million in annual revenue, you should conduct between fifteen and twenty in-person interviews. If you have more than $1 billion in annual revenue, you may need to send out the questionnaire, as it may be too costly to conduct interviews. Survey Monkey is a good choice for passively administering questionnaires. If you are less than $10 million in annual revenue, generating scores with a group of about six people is reasonable.

Who exactly should you interview? Choose middle managers and other senior-level individual contributors from your finance, human resources, operations, and IT departments. We'll call these people your cyber risk "experts." Not because they have deep expertise with cybersecurity but because they know what cyber risk practices are actually happening on your front lines.

You'll choose these experts because junior-level employees will usually lack the necessary perspective to offer valuable insight, and the people at the very top are somewhat disconnected from the day-to-day operations of the company. If your organization is highly dispersed geographically, make sure to interview experts from multiple geographic locations.

## PHASE 1, STEP 4: GENERATE THE QUESTIONNAIRE

The questionnaire that you give your employees during those interviews is the basis for almost all of the data you gather for your cyber risk management game plan. You'll ask your employees a series of questions, all specifically designed to gauge your organization's adherence to the NIST Cybersecurity Framework. As such, the questions will gauge how well you identify, protect, detect, respond to, and recover from cybersecurity risks.

**NIST CYBERSECURITY
FRAMEWORK REFRESHER**

The FTC established the NIST Cybersecurity Framework as a measurement to determine whether your company is practicing reasonable cybersecurity based on five functions:

1. How well you identify digital assets and cyber risks
2. How well you protect your assets against those risks
3. How well you detect cybersecurity breaches
4. How well you respond to those breaches
5. And how well you recover from those breaches

The framework is predicated on the idea that perfect prevention of cyber risks does not exist, so you must have the ability to detect, respond, and recover from data breaches built into your cyber risk management game plan.

Each question in your questionnaire will start with the phrase "How well does your organization..." and the experts will score their response on a scale of zero to ten. Let me tell you how this works.

Most people believe that you can never have too much money. However, it *is* possible to have too much security (or too little).

# How To Measure Security?

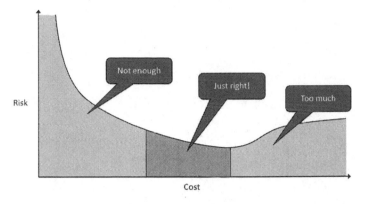

Look at the left side of the diagram. You can see that as you go from left to right along the x-axis, we're spending more money to reduce risk. As you move to the right and enter the green zone, the curve goes lower and risk levels drop to an acceptable level.

As you continue to spend money and add more controls, the risk increases again as you move further to the right. Why is that? Well, past a certain point, your security measures become so difficult to implement that people look for ways to go around them, which creates a false sense of security for the people responsible for managing risk. Plus, you are spending more money than the asset is worth.

Now, let's examine the range of scores respondents will give on your company's security.

Starting on the left, the scores zero through four represent various levels of insecurity, from no security at all to some security.

Scores five through eight represent a range from minimally acceptable security to fully optimized security.

And scores nine and ten represent too much security, which is wasteful of time, money, and morale.

## Possible Scores

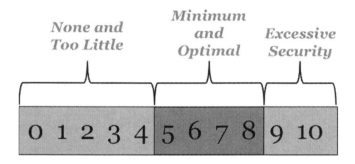

Using these possible scores, we can now create a standard score key to use during the interviews.

| Your Evaluation | Score |
|---|---|
| Our organization rarely or never does this. | o |
| Our organization sometimes does this, but unreliably. Re-work is common. | 3 |
| Our organization does this consistently, with some minor flaws from time-to-time. | 5 |
| Our organization does this consistently with great effectiveness and high quality. | 8 |
| Our organization does this at excessive financial cost. People can't easily get their work done. | 10 |
| I'm not sure if our organization does this or not. | UKN |
| This is not applicable to us. | N/A |

Here's how it works. You start by asking the expert a question such as, "How well has our organization established and implemented the processes to identify, assess, and manage supply chain cybersecurity risks?"

The expert you're interviewing reads the first score statement: "Our organization rarely or never does this," which corresponds with a score of zero. If your expert knows or perceives that your organization is better, then they read the next score statement: "Our organization sometimes does this but unreliably. Rework is common," which corresponds with a score of three.

If your expert knows or perceives that your organization is better than a three, then they read the next score statement and so on until they find a statement that most closely matches their perception. (Of course, they are welcome to choose a value between those shown on the score key.)

Note that there are two other possible responses: "unknown" and "not applicable." Based on how carefully you prepared for the interview, these responses should be rare.

## TOO MUCH CYBERSECURITY

Having too much cybersecurity is like building a $1,000 fence to protect $100 horse. Not only is it unnecessary, but it's too complicated as well. People's productivity will actually decrease with too many cybersecurity controls. If people get frustrated enough, they will stop using your systems and look for work-arounds. For example, if you ask people to remember and manage too many user ID and password combinations, they'll likely just write them down on a Post-It Note and stick it to their monitor. They might just use a personal email account, rather than a hard-to-use company one, to move sensitive information.

Now, you might be wondering how you'll develop the questionnaire. That's exactly why you have me with you on this journey. Here's a list of the thirty-one questions you should use and a brief explanation of each.

Note that each question is categorized by its corresponding activity from the NIST Framework. Furthermore, the activities are each denoted with an identification code in the first column. That identification code tells you which function of the NIST Framework the question relates to and which activity it is examining. For example, the first question has the identification code (ID.AM-1), meaning it relates to the Identify (ID) function of the NIST Framework, and it's examining the Asset Management (AM) activity.

For the rest of the book, I will refer back to these questions by using the codes as shorthand. (Note: Because of the way we've adapted our processes for part 2 for this book, the activity codes you see here are a little different than what you'll see in the NIST Framework, but we expect this will cause you little to no trouble.)

| ACTIVITY | QUESTION | EXPLANATION |
| --- | --- | --- |
| Asset Management (ID.AM-1) | How well are our organization's data, people, devices, systems, and facilities managed according to their relative importance to our *business objectives*? | Assets that are worth more to your *business objectives* deserve more protection than less valuable assets. Prioritize spending this way unless it costs the same to protect all assets as it does to protect only a few high-value ones. |
| Asset Management (ID.AM-2) | How well are our organization's data, people, devices, systems, and facilities managed in accordance with their relative importance to our organization's *cyber risk strategy*? | Assets that help you achieve your *cyber risk strategy* deserve more protection than less valuable assets. Prioritize spending this way unless it costs the same to protect all assets as it does to protect only a few high-value ones. |

| ACTIVITY | QUESTION | EXPLANATION |
|---|---|---|
| Business Environment (ID.BE-1) | How well are our organization's mission, objectives, stakeholders, and activities understood and prioritized so they support our *cybersecurity roles and responsibilities*? | To get the greatest return for your efforts, cybersecurity spending and focus should be prioritized based on what's truly important to your organization and not just on what's easy to do or satisfies a generic checklist. |
| Business Environment (ID.BE-2) | How well are our organization's mission, objectives, stakeholders, and activities understood and prioritized so they support our *cyber risk management decisions*? | To get the greatest return for your efforts, cyber risk decisions must reflect the reality that you need to manage infinite risks with a finite budget. The better organizational priorities are clearly communicated, the more likely the highest and most relevant risks will be well managed. |
| Governance (ID.GV) | How well do our policies, procedures, and processes guide the way we manage cybersecurity risk? | Old, incomplete, or missing documentation often leads to poor or inconsistent cyber risk mitigations. |
| Risk Assessment (ID.RA) | How well does our organization understand the cybersecurity risk to our organization's assets, operations, reputation, and people? | The risks come from both outside and inside your organization and are directed at assets whose value may be perceived differently by attackers than you perceive them. For example, a staff directory may seem ordinary to you, but it is highly sought after by attackers who use the data to plan and execute social engineering attacks. |

| ACTIVITY | QUESTION | EXPLANATION |
|---|---|---|
| Risk Management Strategy (ID.RM) | How well are our organization's priorities, constraints, risk tolerances, and assumptions used to support operational cybersecurity risk decisions? | Executive management must communicate these key inputs to all people who make cyber risk decisions every day; otherwise, the decisions will be inconsistent, and some will be bad for your organization. |
| Supply Chain Risk Management (ID.SC) | How well has our organization established and implemented processes to identify, assess, and manage supply chain cybersecurity risks? | All vendors who play a large role delivering results to customers must be actively included in your cyber risk management activities. |
| Identity Management, Authentication, and Access Control (PR.AC-1) | How well is access to our organization's *physical assets* limited to authorized users, processes, and devices? | People must be identified and allowed to access only those physical assets needed to do their job. For example, access to rooms and storage areas containing personnel records or computer servers should be granted on a need-to-know basis. |
| Identity Management, Authentication, and Access Control (PR.AC-2) | How well is access to our organization's *digital assets* limited to authorized users, processes, and devices? | People must be identified and allowed to access only those digital assets needed to do their job. For example, access to sensitive payroll and customer data should be granted on a need-to-know basis. |
| Awareness and Training (PR.AT-1) | How well are our organization's personnel and partners provided with cybersecurity awareness education? | Everyone in your organization who handles sensitive data and systems must be made aware of the importance of good, ongoing cybersecurity. |

| ACTIVITY | QUESTION | EXPLANATION |
| --- | --- | --- |
| Awareness and Training (PR.AT-2) | How well are our organization's personnel and partners trained to perform their cybersecurity-related duties and responsibilities? | Everyone in your organization who handles sensitive data and systems must be trained so they know how to play their part. |
| Data Security (PR.DS) | How well are our information and records (data) managed to protect the confidentiality, integrity, and availability of information? | These are the basics of good cyberhygiene, the things you do every day to avoid cybersecurity incidents, such as using a high-quality password manager, encrypting data during storage and transfer, and following data protection checklists to prevent costly errors. |
| Information Protection Processes and Procedures (PR.IP) | How well are our security policies, processes, and procedures maintained and used to manage the protection of information systems and assets? | Write down everything important that needs to be done to manage cyber risks so everyone can follow the requirements. |
| Maintenance (PR.MA-1) | How well are the maintenance and repairs of our organization's *industrial control systems* performed consistently with our policies and procedures? | Industrial control systems include computer-controlled thermostats, door access card readers, video surveillance cameras, and lighting. All must be protected against unauthorized access during maintenance. |
| Maintenance (PR.MA-2) | How well are the maintenance and repairs of our organization's *information systems* performed consistent with our policies and procedures? | Information systems include servers, desktops, laptops, mobile devices, and cloud services. All must be protected against unauthorized access during maintenance to guard against data loss or malicious code infection. |

| ACTIVITY | QUESTION | EXPLANATION |
| --- | --- | --- |
| Protective Technology (PR.PT) | How well are our technical security systems managed to ensure the security and resilience of our systems and assets? | Cybersecurity systems (such as antimalware) enforce policies to protect assets and therefore need to be carefully managed. |
| Anomalies and Events (DE.AE-1) | How well is anomalous activity detected in our systems and networks? | In order to know when someone is intruding on your network, it's important to know what kind of traffic is considered to be normal. |
| Anomalies and Events (DE.AE-2) | How well are the potential impacts of security events understood? | Some time must be spent analyzing detected events to know whether an incident has occurred and how impactful it is. |
| Security Continuous Monitoring (DE.CM) | How well are our information systems and assets monitored to identify cybersecurity events and to verify the effectiveness of protective measures? | To keep cyber risk at an acceptable level, you need to watch what's happening to your assets and know about vulnerabilities in your systems. |
| Detection Processes (DE.DP) | How well are our detection processes and procedures maintained and tested to ensure awareness of anomalous events in our systems and networks? | Be clear about who and how detecting is to be done, to include testing detection capabilities, and communicating results to management. |
| Response Planning (RS.RP) | How well are our response processes and procedures executed and maintained, to ensure prompt response to detected cybersecurity incidents? | Preparing in advance to respond to a major incident will increase your chances of minimizing damages. |
| Response Communications (RS.CO-1) | How well are our response activities coordinated with *internal stakeholders*, such as executive management? | To understand how your organization is affected, incident reports need to be made clear to management and shared on a need-to-know and timely basis with *insiders*. |

| ACTIVITY | QUESTION | EXPLANATION |
|---|---|---|
| Response Communications (RS.CO-2) | How well are our response activities coordinated with *external stakeholders*, such as law enforcement agencies? | To understand how your organization is affected and to make our online community safer, incident reports need to be made clear and shared on a need-to-know and timely basis with selected *outsiders*. |
| Response Analysis (RS.AN) | How well does our organization analyze past incidents to ensure effective response and support recovery activities? | Past notifications from detection systems need to be investigated and understood to improve response strategies. |
| Response Mitigation (RS.MI) | How well does our organization prevent the spread of a cybersecurity event, mitigate its effects, and resolve the incident? | When incidents happen, they need to be stopped from spreading and kept from happening again. And newly identified vulnerabilities need to be either fixed or documented as accepted risks. |
| Response Improvements (RS.IM) | How well does our organization improve our response activities by incorporating lessons learned from current and previous incidents? | Because cyberattackers innovate all the time, we need to be regularly improving too. |
| Recovery Planning (RC.RP) | How well does our organization use recovery processes and procedures to ensure restoration of systems or assets affected by cybersecurity incidents? | Preparing in advance to recover after a major incident will increase your chances of quickly returning to normal. |
| Recovery Improvements (RC.IM) | How well does our organization improve our recovery planning and processes by incorporating lessons learned into future activities? | Because cyberattackers innovate all the time, we need to be regularly improving too. |

| ACTIVITY | QUESTION | EXPLANATION |
| --- | --- | --- |
| Recovery Communications (RC.CO-1) | How well does our organization coordinate restoration activities with internal stakeholders, such as executive management? | To return to normal quickly, *insiders* need to be kept informed as the recovery continues. |
| Recovery Communications (RC.CO-2) | How well does our organization coordinate restoration activities with external parties, such as cyberincident coordinating centers, Internet service providers, owners of attacking systems, victims, other Computer Security Incident Response Teams (CSIRTs), and vendors? | To return to normal quickly and protect the online community, *outsiders* need to be kept informed as the recovery continues. |

Our online Cyber Risk Workbook includes a useful version of this questionnaire in a Google Sheets format. The workbook contains a model questionnaire that you can copy as many times as you like, along with sample data, reporting, graphing, and other functionalities that you'll read about in the rest of this book. You can access it here: http://b.link/cyber-risk-workbook.

## PHASE 1, STEP 5: DETERMINE YOUR TARGET SCORES

Now that you know which questions you'll ask and how the zero-to-ten scoring system works, your next step is to determine your specific targets within the five-to-eight range. Your company is unique, and so are your cyber risk needs. Therefore, you will want to prioritize certain aspects of cybersecurity over others.

You'll do this for each of the five functions in the NIST Framework:

- Identify
- Protect
- Detect
- Respond
- Recover

Using the zero-to-ten score key, a five is a minimum acceptable score while an eight is fully optimized. But you can choose any number you think is appropriate and reasonable. Let's discuss your options.

## MINIMUM SCORE APPROACH

Setting out to achieve a minimum score across the board is reasonable, depending on your industry, customer expectations, and your organization's maturity.

# Target Scores—Minimum

| Acme Corporation | Target |
|:---:|:---:|
| IDENTIFY (ID) | 5.0 |
| PROTECT (PR) | 5.0 |
| DETECT (DE) | 5.0 |
| RESPOND (RS) | 5.0 |
| RECOVER (RC) | 5.0 |

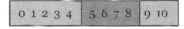

0 1 2 3 4 5 6 7 8 9 10

STRONG CASTLE APPROACH

Another approach is what I call the strong castle. This target score profile is still the current practice of many organizations across many industries. The idea is to know where your "crown jewels" are and put lots of protection on them.

# Target Scores—Strong Castle

| Acme Corporation | Target |
|---|---|
| IDENTIFY (ID) | 5.0 |
| PROTECT (PR) | 7.0 |
| DETECT (DE) | 5.0 |
| RESPOND (RS) | 5.0 |
| RECOVER (RC) | 5.0 |

| 0 1 2 3 4 | 5 6 7 8 | 9 10 |
|---|---|---|

Done well, this strategy should minimize the need to have optimal cybersecurity in the other functions since you've already assumed that only minor incidents would occur. As previously discussed, cyberattackers have become very effective at compromising people rather than just our technology, so this strategy doesn't work as well as it used to. Imagine a medieval castle. When it was built, it could withstand any attack currently available to its occupants' enemies: arrows, battering rams, swords, and so forth. But as the weapons progressed, a castle could no longer withstand any attack. Could you imagine a castle surviving a drone missile attack? Not likely. That's what it's like trying to take a strong-castle approach to cybersecurity.

## FIRST RESPONDER APPROACH

Another approach is called the first responder. Here's that target score profile:

# Target Scores—First Responder

| Acme Corporation | Target |
|:---:|:---:|
| IDENTIFY (ID) | 5.0 |
| PROTECT (PR) | 5.0 |
| DETECT (DE) | 5.0 |
| RESPOND (RS) | 8.0 |
| RECOVER (RC) | 5.0 |

| 0 1 2 3 4 | 5 6 7 8 | 9 10 |
|:---:|:---:|:---:|

Having your Respond function target score as an eight is a benefit because a fast, high-quality response will mitigate having relatively lower target scores in the other four functions.

BIG CITY APPROACH

An approach that's appropriate for a larger company is called the big city. Here's that target score profile:

# Target Scores—Big City

| Acme Corporation | Target |
|:---:|:---:|
| IDENTIFY (ID) | 5.0 |
| PROTECT (PR) | 5.0 |
| DETECT (DE) | 5.0 |
| RESPOND (RS) | 8.0 |
| RECOVER (RC) | 8.0 |

| 0 1 2 3 4 | 5 6 7 8 | 9 10 |
|:---:|:---:|:---:|

A very mature perspective on cybersecurity is to see your company's data network more as a modern city than as a medieval fortress. You need a police force, fire department, and transportation department that can rapidly deploy when trouble erupts (Respond). Supportive services enable fast cleanup and repair (Recover). Like a big American city, there are no gates, so anyone can come in. Therefore, you need to respond to and recover from problems fast to get the city moving again.

WORLD CLASS APPROACH

Finally, here's the world class target score profile:

# Target Scores—World Class

| Acme Corporation | Target |
|:---:|:---:|
| IDENTIFY (ID) | 8.0 |
| PROTECT (PR) | 8.0 |
| DETECT (DE) | 8.0 |
| RESPOND (RS) | 8.0 |
| RECOVER (RC) | 8.0 |

| 0 1 2 3 4 | 5 6 7 8 | 9 10 |
|:---:|:---:|:---:|

Being world class at cyber risk management is very expensive and difficult. Oddly, it's only practical for either very small organizations or a government operation, such as the NSA, that can spend whatever is needed to achieve this level of cybersecurity.

If you are an executive manager of a software as a service business with $10 million in annual revenue, you likely maintain records of many sensitive digital assets of your customers, including mailing addresses and credit card information. You also have source code and other trade secrets. As a result, you may want to focus on targeting a six or seven on the Protect function, while targeting a five on the other four functions.

In contrast, if you are the manager of a geographically distributed division in an $800 million company, the big city profile might be a better fit.

Regardless of the reasoning, choose your target score for each of the five NIST Framework functions and record them before you begin the interview process.

## PHASE 1, STEP 6: CONDUCT THE INTERVIEWS

It might be tempting to send the thirty-one-item questionnaire to your employees in a mass email, but that is not ideal. The best way to conduct the interviews is by doing them in person with a select group on an individual level. Here's a sample invitation (feel free to use the materials at the links):

The very process of asking these questions is a marvelous training opportunity for the interviewee because most people don't know the definition of good cyber risk management and have therefore never even considered measuring it. And it's best if you're not the one conducting the interviews either. Have a very well-respected senior employee or a neutral outsider conduct the interviews.

## TOO MANY PEOPLE, NOT ENOUGH TIME

One of my employees spent twenty-two hours over two weeks at a $300 million company interviewing experts from ten different departments. These interviews were conducted face-to-face, either in person or over video, and were scheduled back to back in four-hour blocks, with a short break for the interviewer somewhere near the midpoint of each block.

Why do I tell you this information? To help you understand what kind of time commitment the data-gathering portion of this method requires. You need to understand the kind of resource commitment I'm talking about.

Now, your company may be a size that won't accommodate in-person interviews with every single person. In that case, you can choose department heads and other managerial staff to be interviewed on an individual basis and then send the email version of the questionnaire to everyone else *after* the in-person interviews.

If you've never done anything like this before, the entire process of setting up and conducting all the interviews will take approximately one hundred hours. If you choose to use us at Cyber Risk Opportunities, these interviews would take approximately fifty hours, and we take care of all preparation and scoring.

During the interview, give each interviewee a printed score key. That way, when you ask them each of the thirty-one questions out loud, they can easily choose the score that best reflects their experiences in your company. Moreover, having the scoring table on hand helps to keep your respondents' answers uniform, thus giving you more reliable data.

## THE POTENTIAL FLAWS OF THE IN-PERSON INTERVIEWS

Plenty of people criticize this interview approach, arguing that your employees won't tell the whole truth out of fear of retribution and that your questionnaire results will always be biased. That is a valid criticism.

Biases are inevitable for any kind of data collection. Our approach does a reasonable job of moderating that bias, and actually, we've found that people are *more* likely to give accurate scores in person than someone who fills out a questionnaire by themselves. In fact, there are so many well-known biases when people complete questionnaires alone that Survey Monkey includes many features to increase the quality of survey data. That's why we encourage you to use Survey Monkey if your organization is so big that it prohibits in-person interviews.

Again, nothing about cybersecurity is perfect. You just do the best you can to manage risks. The same applies to the interviews. They won't be perfect, but you will do everything in your power to mitigate biases.

## SETTING PROPER EXPECTATIONS

When a large corporation becomes fixed in one way of doing business and the world around it changes, it often experiences a crisis and must force a change in order to survive. That change may come in the form of strengthening their cybersecurity, or it may mean they discontinue entire product lines.

IBM went through a seminal change like this in the early 1990s. They used to be a big hardware manufacturer, but once they realized the future of their company was in providing services, they changed not only *what* they sold, but they also changed the very skillsets they chose to focus on (service rather than hardware). Companies that endure the test of time know how to change themselves; otherwise, they get stale and go bankrupt. Kodak, for example, which was founded in 1888, had to file for Chapter 11 bankruptcy protection in 2012 because of the decline in photographic film sales and the company's slowness in transitioning to digital photography.

When an executive embarks on the task of changing their company—modernizing their organization, changing its culture, and changing the way it thinks about its customers, its products, and how it is relevant—it can be overwhelming for the employees if you don't actively manage the organizational changes you're undertaking.

People in your company may resist the changes you're making to your cybersecurity. The best way to overcome that resistance is to reiterate that this is a team sport you're all playing and that everybody will have a role. The tone of the interviews should be a mix of candid and respectful. And keep it moving at a good pace.

So encourage them to be forthright in their responses.

Make sure the scores they give will remain confidential: no particular scores or comments will be attributed to any named individuals. If they think a score should be zero, then they should say zero. If they want to explain why they gave that score, allow them to speak their mind. That data may become invaluable.

Another key component to gathering the best data is to show them as much information as possible to understand what to expect in the interview room. For a start, send them to the following URL, where Cyber Risk Opportunities has a short video that helps explain the scoring and interview process: http://b.link/interview.

I advise that you *do not* give your interviewees the questions in advance. For this step, I believe the best scores come from the gut, not from long, deliberative consideration.

## THE INTERVIEW AGENDA

The first ten minutes of the actual interview should be a recap of everything I have already explained. Whoever is conducting the interview should remind the expert that this is a management improvement effort, not an outside audit. Encourage them to be candidly respectful with their responses, then ask if they have any questions about the zero-to-ten scoring scale. Find out if they had a chance to watch the video at the link I provided. If they didn't watch it, give them the score key and a brief explanation of the scoring process and purpose of this interview. If they have watched the video, proceed to the interview.

> Whoever is conducting the interview will record all of the respondent answers in a spreadsheet, with each interviewee organized by department, which allows you to isolate scores by department. Use the Cyber Risk Workbook we provide here or create your own: http://b.link/cyber-risk-workbook.

Now, the tempo of the interview should be very brisk—less than an hour per interviewee. Do not ask the interviewee to elaborate on their scores, but if they do feel compelled to provide justification, be sure to record those answers in the spreadsheet. They will become helpful in phase 2 of the process.

These should not be long, grueling interviews. You and the expert both want to get in, get the scores, and get out. That is the most respectful way to conduct these interviews, and interviewees will leave feeling good if you handle it that way. They will feel that you've respected their time and their expertise.

As the interviews progress, you may encounter some respondents who say they don't know anything about cybersecurity. In response, tell them that that may be true, but that they are an expert in their own department and that they know more about that department's practices than anyone else outside of it. Reiterate that you want to hear their opinion, even if it's based on a perception or only partial information.

When it comes to change management, if people are uncomfortable with the change you're proposing, it's very important for them to feel heard, even if they're nervous about sharing their opinions. If you listen to them up front, it goes a long way toward getting their buy-in on a continuous basis.

## PHASE 1, STEP 7: COMPILE AND AVERAGE THE SCORES

Once you've completed all of the interviews and recorded the scores, your next step is to average them out and compare them to your target scores for each Activity of the NIST Framework.

Using the downloadable Cyber Risk Workbook (http.//b. link/cyber-risk-workbook), where all target scores have been set to six, here is an example radar diagram showing results:

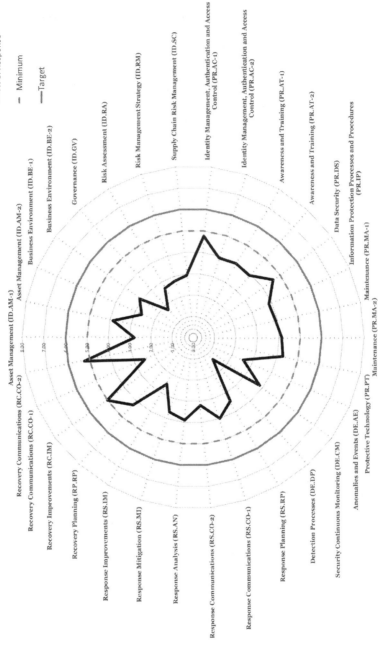

The radar diagram is useful for seeing the big picture of where you are (as represented by the Average Response category) compared to the Minimum and Target scores.

Again, using the downloadable Cyber Risk Workbook (http://b.link/cyber-risk-workbook), here are the top five cyber risks in the sample data set.

| ACTIVITY | QUESTION | AVG. RESPONSE | MIN | TARGET | GAP |
|---|---|---|---|---|---|
| Detection Processes (DE.DP) | How well are our detection processes and procedures maintained and tested to ensure awareness of anomalous events in our systems and networks? | 1.4 | 5 | 6 | 4.6 |
| Governance (ID.GV) | How well do our policies, procedures, and processes guide the way we manage cybersecurity risk? | 1.8 | 5 | 6 | 4.2 |
| Response Improvements (RS.IM) | How well does our organization improve our response activities by incorporating lessons learned from current and previous incidents? | 2.5 | 5 | 6 | 3.5 |
| Recovery Communications (RC.CO-1) | How well does our organization coordinate restoration activities with internal stakeholders, such as executive management? | 2.5 | 5 | 6 | 3.5 |
| Anomalies and Events (DE.AE) | How well is anomalous activity detected in our systems and networks? | 2.6 | 5 | 6 | 3.4 |

Notice this list is in order of gap size (rightmost column) and includes activities from the Detect, Identify, Response, and Recover functions. Why is Protect not in the top five? In my experience, most companies are underinvested in all of the functions except Protect.

That doesn't mean the Protect function is meeting or exceeding targets, but it does mean that your biggest cybersecurity gaps likely exist elsewhere.

## CENTRALIZED OR DECENTRALIZED?

How you manage cyber risks depends a lot on your organizational model. Here's an example.

One of our customers is a mortgage broker with a single corporate office and nearly fifty branches spread across the country. With their decentralized business model, each branch is a locally owned and independently operated subsidiary. As a result, hiring, firing, and other business decisions are made on a local level—including IT support. They decide on a branch by-branch basis whether they even hire any IT people. A new employee would have their user account created and managed by their local office.

On the other hand, a highly centralized company— with one main office—is more likely to have an entire IT department that handles most of the cybersecurity work. A new employee at that kind of company will likely have their new user account created and managed by the central IT team.

This means when you are closing your gaps, you may have to make changes in only one place if you have a strong central office. Or if you are in a highly decentralized model, you may need to persuade each branch manager to make a change.

Whichever situation you find yourself in, be sure to create a change management approach that best fits.

## PHASE 1, STEP 8: COMMUNICATE YOUR TOP FIVE CYBER RISKS

At this point, phase 1 is almost over. If your results don't meet your expectations, you may want to ask your experts for more details to help you understand why your actual scores were so far off from your target scores.

In general, though, your work in phase 1 is done. The only thing left to do is look at the data and see what stories they tell you. Two common themes often emerge: most companies are strongest in the Protect function—because that's where most organizations invest their time and energy—and they are weakest in Detect and Recover.

Why is that? Historically, cyber risks have been perceived as technology problems alone. Therefore, IT departments are measured by their ability to keep tech services up and running. As a result, they are great at detecting *outages*, but they don't spend nearly enough energy detecting violations of sensitive data.

Moreover, organizations tend to be weak in the Recover function because most companies are not accustomed to having their technological failures laid bare in the public eye, so they haven't developed an internal capacity to explain to outsiders why their technology has failed. As a result, most crisis situations are handled by the marketing department, who don't know how to communicate technical breakdowns and data breaches to the public.

Which brings me to the final point of this chapter: you may find that your target scores are so far off because your perception of your top cyber risks are heavily informed by fear-mongering headlines and stories from your vendors.

You may notice that nowhere in the questionnaire do we ask about firewalls. This is because we're approaching cyber as a business risk, not a strictly technological risk. You still need a great set of firewalls, antispam filters, and so forth. But our process is designed to help you practice reasonable cybersecurity in a world where technological defenses alone will not set you up for success.

Unfortunately, the headlines of major cybersecurity breaches—like the one at Yahoo—and the marketing copy from vendors trying to sell you a product don't tell the full story. You have your scores from your questionnaires. You have the full story *for your company*, and that's what matters.

# PHASE 2

## ORGANIZATIONAL HANDWASHING

AsusTek is a computer hardware company that makes gear for personal computers. In 2016, they learned of some vulnerabilities in their routers, but instead of forthrightly disclosing the vulnerability, they hid it from their consumers and continued selling the defective—and, frankly, dangerous—routers. As a result, hackers located these routers and exploited them to gain access to more than 12,900 connected storage devices.

AsusTek didn't notify their consumers or their retailers because they were concerned that if they did, their reputation would be diminished in the marketplace, which would negatively impact their sales. What always happens in these situations is that someone finds the defect anyway, and rather than the company being in control of the story, the disgruntled consumers control the narrative, which hurts the company's sales even more in the long run.

If you disclose the vulnerability yourself, you control the narrative. In fact, you not only control the narrative, but you also actually create tremendous trust with your consumers. For example, if AsusTek had made a public announcement saying, "We are very sorry. We have identified a problem with our routers, and here is our solution to remedy the problem," it would have actually been a brand-enhancing maneuver.

People love that authenticity and vulnerability. That announcement might have resulted in a decrease in sales for a short time, but over the long haul, it would have enhanced their reputation, not diminished it. They would have become known as the straight-talkers of cybersecurity, and people would want to buy their products—not because they'd expect them to be flawless, but because they would know that when a flaw is discovered, they will be up front about it.

That's what you should strive for with your cyber risk management game plan—not to create perfectly secure products or practice perfect cybersecurity but to practice reasonable measures to ensure that cyberattacks don't happen, and when they do, you recover quickly and are forthright to your customers.

Want an example of someone who did this well? Home Depot in 2014. Their data breach included 56 million stolen credit card records from their customers. Whereas Target experienced a similar breach in 2013—when 40 million records were stolen—Home Depot didn't face nearly as much criticism as Target, despite similarities between the breaches. How were they similar?

- The customer's credit card information was stolen as they paid for their purchase.
- Both were compromised by outsiders through a third-party vendor.
- In each case, the attackers inserted malicious code into the card readers undetected.
- Both were exploited during their most important shopping season.

A big reason Target faced greater criticism than Home Depot was because they waited a full week to inform customers of the breach, whereas Home Depot notified their customers *even before they had fully confirmed the breach:* "We apologize to our customers for the inconvenience and anxiety this has caused and want to reassure them that they will not be liable for fraudulent charges," said Frank Blake, Home Depot's chairman and CEO.

The difference in response shows in the financial consequences each company faced: Home Depot's data breach cost it $179 million versus Target's $292 million (plus, Target CEO Gregg Steinhafel lost his job after thirty-five years with the company).

Data breaches happen even if you implement every facet of this cyber risk management game plan. How you respond to the data breaches is the key determinant of your ability to recover from them with as little damage to your business and reputation as possible.

## THOUGHTS ON CYBER RISK MANAGEMENT

Before we talk about how to manage your top cyber risks, I want to share some key success factors.

### PRIORITY IS CRUCIAL

Just like every other executive, you face an infinite number of cyber risks. Yet you, like everyone else, have a finite amount of resources to use on cyber risk management. That means you need to make tough choices about which risks to manage and which to accept.

It's not an easy problem to solve.

Prioritization is the best way to deal with this impossible

situation. Just as we prioritized your cyber risks, I'll show you how to prioritize your mitigations. While prioritization is not a guarantee that you'll never get exploited, it's a reasonable way to address this difficult problem.

The challenge for most people is to trust their prioritization and actually implement the plan. You will hear lots of reasons from other people about why your prioritization is wrong. Listen to the criticism, but don't be too quick to change course once you set off. As you'll see in phase 3, there is a built-in mechanism to make course corrections.

## GIVE EVERYONE A ROLE

Everyone needs a role in your new risk management game plan. As an executive, you have to look at every job description and ask yourself what you can reasonably add in order to spread the cybersecurity work around. Then, once you've made that change, ask yourself if those new roles will require additional tools. If people don't already have a cybersecurity-related responsibility, you need to set them up for success once you add that new responsibility to their plate.

If you're asking everyone in the customer service department to use unique passwords for every job-related account they use, you can't just tell them to figure it out themselves. Systematize it for them. First, put it in the job description that they must protect company accounts, then set them all up with the same high-quality password manager with centralized reporting. That way, you can access a single console to see how many people on your customer service team are actively using it. If they are not actively using the password manager, they are not only practicing poor cyberhygiene, but they are also violating their job description.

### ADMIN ACCESS AT TWITTER

In 2011, the FTC alleged that Twitter gave almost all its employees administrative control over the system. By providing administrative access to so many employees, Twitter increased the risk that a compromise of any of its employees' credentials could result in a serious breach to all of their users.

Administrative control should be granted very selectively. The more people who have and use admin accounts for reading email and browsing the web, the more likely you'll have a cybersecurity incident.

### THE CHALLENGE OF SCALE

On an individual basis, the changes you implement as part of your cyber risk management game plan are simple and straightforward. In fact, for a change such as adding a line to every job description, you'll hand that off to your management team. As you continue to find ways to improve on those thirty-one questions, you will have to make potentially large-scale changes across the company.

If you asked a single person on your customer service team to get a password manager for all of their accounts, they would simply install a password manager and figure it out within a matter of days. And if they didn't meet that objective quickly, it wouldn't take you much time at all to check that individual's progress. However, when you roll out your changes across a large organization of people, you experience an increase in complexity, cost, and time investment. The larger the organization, the more difficult it is to scale each element of your game plan.

## KEEP IT SIMPLE

The complexity of change, along with unclear priorities and benefits, is what keeps most executives from making improvements to their cybersecurity. They become overwhelmed with the scale of this change. The benefit of the methodology in this book is that it prioritizes and focuses you. In the examples below, you will see the best way to implement changes to your cybersecurity in a way that is highly focused and simple.

By being laser-focused, it reduces the complexity to the minimum necessary in order to hit your target scores. That's where the data you collected in phase 1 becomes significant. If your staff doesn't believe they need to add more security measures, you can simply show them the numbers that *they gave you*.

## DELIBERATE RATE OF CHANGE

Later on, when you are implementing your game plan, be sure not to overwhelm your workforce with changes. I'm sure you've seen that happen before with other improvement programs, such as switching out your accounting software or email system. You'll need to carefully sequence the changes required by your cyber risk mitigations at a rate they can handle alongside all the other changes going on in their world. Only you can know what the right rate is.

But there is good news: not all of your mitigations will require active changes from your staff. Some, as you will see, will be transparent to them, and those can be rolled out in conjunction with the more impactful changes.

### IT'S TIME TO DEVELOP YOUR GAME PLAN

Now that you have a prioritized list of your top five cybersecurity risks, it's time to develop your cyber risk management game plan. As I mentioned earlier, this second phase takes place over the course of thirty days.

I don't expect you to actively manage every cyber risk facing your company. In fact, if you do nothing more than work through the questionnaires and identify your risks, you will be far ahead of your competition, who has probably not done anything similar.

This is the point in the process where it's useful to work under attorney-client privilege as a way to protect yourself in case your risks manifest themselves differently than you expected. If one of your cyber risks ends up being the source of a data breach in the future and you didn't prioritize it in your cyber risk management game plan, you could be accused of knowing that risk existed but not taking action. This could lead to a charge of negligence in a court of law, to say nothing of the court of public opinion. By conducting this work under attorney-client privilege, you are protected.

## CONTRACTUAL FIREWALLS

Before we go any further in this sidebar, remember that I'm a cybersecurity practitioner, not a lawyer. Please speak with a lawyer to get specific advice for your situation.

Most organizations make use of vendors to deliver products and services. Your credit card processor is a common example. But if your vendor causes a large cyber failure, such as a long outage or a breach of sensitive information, your reputation and your customers will suffer.

So both your vendors and customers should be told what you expect them to do to protect against, and ultimately deal with, cyber failures. Setting these expectations using carefully written contract language indemnifies you against excessive financial losses, which creates a contractual firewall for your organization. (By the way, the word "indemnify" means "to compensate someone for harm or loss.")

You'll set expectations with your vendors in a master services agreement or similar contract. There are two primary points you'll want to make. First, both parties will share responsibility for data security. Second, include an indemnification provision that describes who's financially responsible in the case of cybersecurity failure along with the limits of that responsibility. If the vendor is responsible for a failure, require them to cover your costs of liability, legal defense, and crisis management for both first-party and third-party costs.

To set expectations with customers, limit your liability in the case of cybersecurity failure. Make sure your service offerings are "as is" and your liability is limited to the amount customers actually paid.

## PHASE 2, STEP 1: PLUG THE GAPS

Start by looking at your number one risk and asking yourself, "Why is there a gap between our actual scores and our target scores?"

Ask yourself what you would have to do to get that score to your target. You don't have to purchase world-class cybersecurity protection capabilities to reach a 5.0. You simply need to do whatever's reasonable for your organization. That's your baseline question for allocating resources to manage your cyber risks: What does my company need to do in order to reach our target?

Looking back at the top five cyber risks from chapter 5, let's explore how you might close the gaps for your top two cyber risks:

| ACTIVITY | QUESTION | AVG. RESPONSE | MIN | TARGET | GAP |
|---|---|---|---|---|---|
| Detection Processes (DE.DP) | How well are our detection processes and procedures maintained and tested to ensure awareness of anomalous events in our systems and networks? | 1.4 | 5 | 6 | 4.6 |
| Governance (ID.GV) | How well do our policies, procedures, and processes guide the way we manage cyber-security risk? | 1.8 | 5 | 6 | 4.2 |

In both cases, the average score was between 1 and 2. When you look at the score key, you can see they are somewhere between "Our organization rarely or never does this" (a zero) and "Our organization sometimes does this but unreliably" (a three). In short, it looks grim. Anytime you score less than a five, it's a serious failing on the part of your cybersecurity process.

On the bright side in this example, whatever processes are already in place for detection processes and governance are probably not worth keeping. That means a completely fresh start. Because the cybersecurity landscape changes so quickly, building a new cyber risk process can be easier and more successful than remodeling an old one.

## CASE STUDY IN THE IDENTIFY FUNCTION

One of our customers had a low score in the Identify function, due in large part to their low scores in response to the following question: "How well are your organization's mission, objectives, stakeholders, and activities understood and prioritized so that they support your cybersecurity roles, responsibilities, and risk management decisions?"

They started by looking at their job descriptions and realized that the only people who had cybersecurity roles and responsibilities were their IT staff. None of their other stakeholders felt it was part of their job description to identify cyber risks. Their score was below a five.

Because of their new knowledge of the NIST Framework, they knew this was inadequate. Every stakeholder needed to share in the responsibility to be cybersecure. As a result, they added a new line to every job description that said, "Must follow company procedures to identify and report potential breaches to sensitive customer data." It was a seemingly small change, but it was enough to increase their score, improve their Identify function, and enhance their practice of reasonable cybersecurity.

## CLOSING THE DETECTION PROCESSES GAP

When you look inside the NIST Framework at the details under Detection Processes (DE.DP), you will see the following five requirements. (We routinely turn the NIST statements into questions to make our work easier.)

- DE.DP-1: How well does our organization define

roles and responsibilities to detect cyber incidents to ensure accountability?

- DE.DP-2: How well do our organization's cyber incident detection activities comply with all applicable legal, regulatory, and customer requirements?
- DE.DP-3: How well does our organization regularly test cyber incident detection processes and procedures?
- DE.DP-4: How well does our organization communicate cyber incident detection information to appropriate internal and external parties?
- DE.DP-5: How well does our organization regularly review and improve cyber incident detection processes?

Now, in order to hit your target score of six, you need to examine each question and figure out how to make sure each requirement can be satisfied at a level of six. When you are done making improvements, you need to be able to say for each one, "Our organization does this consistently, with few minor flaws."

Coming up with the specific steps for making improvements requires specialized skills. Don't expect to figure it all out on your own. You will need help. Moreover, your company requires customization for your particular security systems and business model. For those and other reasons, I can't give you a "set it and forget it" answer to improve each activity, but here are starting points for three of them:

- DE.DP-2: Conduct an annual management review to identify and understand all legal, regulatory, and customer requirements regarding cyber incident detection. Use a requirements traceability matrix to demonstrate compliance.
- DE.DP-3: Conduct brief, quarterly tests of cyber incident detection processes against a serious, likely scenario. Do this as a tabletop exercise, if necessary.
- DE.DP-5: Conduct an effectiveness review of your cyber incident detection processes every six months and make improvements as needed.

Before we drill deeper into how to get access to the specialized skills needed to close your gaps, let's take a look at closing the gap for the number two cyber risk in our example; governance.

## CLOSING THE GOVERNANCE GAP

When you look inside the NIST Framework at the details under Governance (ID.GV), you will see the following six requirements:

- ID.GV-1: How well does our organization establish information security policies?

- ID.GV-2-a: How well does our organization incorporate cybersecurity roles and responsibilities into staff position descriptions?
- ID.GV-2-b: How well does our organization incorporate cybersecurity roles and responsibilities into vendor contracts?
- ID.GV-3: How well does our organization understand and satisfy our legal and regulatory cybersecurity requirements (e.g, privacy, data breach notifications laws, PCI, HIPAA, GLBA, GDPR, FRPA, FISM, DFARS, etc.)?
- ID.GV-4-a: How well does our organization put all the necessary people, processes, and technologies in place to address governance of cybersecurity?
- ID.GV-4-b: How well does our organization put all the necessary people, processes, and technologies in place to address cybersecurity risk management?

As before, in order to hit the target score of six, you need to examine each question and figure out how to make sure each requirement can be satisfied at the six level. But notice that these questions are not as technical in nature compared to the Detection Processes questions. In fact, you should require little to no help from a skilled IT or cybersecurity expert to close the governance gaps. Rather, you will need assistance from Human Resources, Legal, Contracting, and your peer executives to sort this all out.

See why I keep saying cybersecurity is a team sport?

Because the nature of this section is rooted in management rather than technology, I can offer you the following starting points for the first four requirements:

- ID.GV-1: Review your security policy annually and train all staff annually. Review one time with outside counsel who is an expert at FTC "reasonableness" standards.
- ID.GV-2-a: Revise all staff position descriptions to incorporate information security roles and responsibilities and inform all staff of changes.
- ID.GV-2-b: Add new requirements in vendor and consultant contracts describing how they should protect your regulated and high-value information and systems.
- ID.GV-3: Conduct an annual legal review to identify and understand all legal and regulatory cybersecurity requirements.

## IN-HOUSE VERSUS OUTSOURCING

These days, cybersecurity experts are in high demand, and research shows that trend will continue for years to come. By 2021, there will be 3.5 million cybersecurity job openings. Why? The sources of cybersecurity talent have been unable to keep pace with the dramatic rise in cybercrime, which is predicted to cost the world $6 trillion annually by 2021, up from $3 trillion in 2015.

Particularly rare are the people who understand and practice the major point I'm making in this book: cyber risks are a business risk just as serious and worthy of executive attention as risks to sales, order fulfillment, and accounts receivable. This means it may be difficult to hire the talented cybersecurity people you want on your team. Even if you can find them, they will be expensive. Not only that, but odds are, they will receive frequent, unsolicited job offers from organizations willing to pay more than you are.

For example, here in the Seattle area, there are many large, growing employers in the technology industry that are paying very high compensation for experienced cybersecurity people. That makes it difficult for smaller, nontechnical organizations to hire and retain the cybersecurity staffers they need. Some of the struggling organizations are opening smaller offices in other cities or countries to find the talent they need. Or they are outsourcing.

This means you need to be very smart about where to get the talent you need to execute your cyber risk mitigation plans. Here's my advice:

1. If you already have a smart cybersecurity expert on your team, do whatever you can to keep them! That means regular training and task assignments that hold their interest.

2. Be thoughtful about which work you want to keep in-house versus outsourced. My rule of thumb on this is to keep the work that is core to your business in the hands of insiders. In contrast, there are lots of tasks that are good candidates for outsourcing to another company.

3. Here are three categories of tasks into which you can sort the work:

   A. Core—The employees in this position should be doing tasks that:
      - Help the business take smart cyber risks
      - Deliver higher quality cybersecurity decisions than outsiders
      - Establish and maintain critical business relationships with people across the company so the cybersecurity agenda gets the attention it deserves

   B. Strategic Outsource—The employees are directly assisted by outside experts who do the majority (60%-80%) of the detailed work.

   C. Commodity Outsource—Outsiders doing all (100%) the work under direct oversight of your employee.

Here's how you might implement this approach. (I'm not suggesting you do all of these items. They are just examples.)

*Core Tasks*

These tasks should be performed by a person qualified to work as a project manager, preferably with IT security knowledge and experience, which can be learned.

With a tight labor market and typical emphasis on providing internal opportunities to existing employees, first try to recruit a current employee.

Here are the core tasks to be done by the project manager:

- Committee work
  - Chair the Cyber Risk Committee
  - Participate on the Change Control Committee
  - Participate on the Disaster Recovery Committee
- Standards and procedure development and maintenance
- Prepare for and support the annual external audits
- Support annual cyberinsurance renewal
- Conduct informal assessments as needed
- Support disaster-recovery exercises and updates to plans
- Act as incident management for disaster recovery

- Manage cross-functional cybersecurity projects
- Collaborate with business and technology leaders to deliver proper separation of duties within enterprise applications
- Support annual cybersecurity audit compliance activities
- Remain current on best cybersecurity practices for your industry

*Strategic Tasks Ideal to Outsource*

- Policy development and quarterly maintenance
- Annual company cyber risk assessment
- High-risk security assessments
- Annual firewall effectiveness assessments
- Third-party cyber risk assessments
- Technical vulnerability assessments
- Digital forensics in support of incident management
- Annual update to emergency preparedness program
- Annual review of compliance with existing policies and procedures
- Evaluate open source threat intelligence
- Report on the results of network intrusion detection activities

*Commodity Tasks Ideal to Outsource*

- Conduct network intrusion detection activities

- Education and awareness training
- Administrate antiphishing training program
- Perform periodic cybersecurity controls reviews
- Conduct cybersecurity reviews of current and prospective systems, applications, and external vendors
- Perform periodic reviews of other controls, such as:
  - Annual user account reconciliation
  - Semiannual vendor and third-party cybersecurity assessments
  - Quarterly physical security access review to data center
  - Monthly reviews of
    A. Employee termination-to-account deactivation
    B. Oracle privileged access
    C. Microsoft privileged access
    D. Linux privileged access

## COST ESTIMATION

Whether you keep cybersecurity services in-house or outsourced, you still have to calculate the cost of implementation. When we estimate costs as part of cyber risk management planning, we like to estimate the three-year total cost of ownership (3TCO) for each mitigation. This helps better compare the costs of different mitigations. Why? Because some mitigations are heavy on one-time costs, while others are cheap to start but cost a lot to keep running. And some mitigations just cost a lot all the time.

The formula for 3TCO is:

(Implementation Cost) + (Annual Operating Cost × 3)

Each of these two major 3TCO components has a breakdown calculation. For Implementation Cost, it's:

(Acquisition Cost) + (Implementation Hours × Labor Cost)

When we don't know in advance who will do the work, we use a labor cost of $125 per hour. This is a blended rate between the inside cost of labor ($75 per hour) and the outside cost of labor ($175 per hour). Of course, be sure to use current rates for your market. Once it's clear who will do the work, then we update our cost estimate. Use your own estimates for the labor costs in your market.

For Annual Operating Cost, the formula is:

(Annual Renewal Cost) + (Operating Hours × Labor Cost)

How does this look in practice? Here's an example: suppose you need to implement a new security event log management system that will help improve your ability to quickly detect cybersecurity incidents. The various cost factors might look like this:

| AQC. COST | IMPL. HOURS | LABOR RATE | TOTAL IMPL. COST | ANNUAL RENEW $ | OPER- ATING HRS/YR | LABOR RATE | OPERAT- ING $/YR | 3TCO |
|---|---|---|---|---|---|---|---|---|
| $36,000 | 80 | $125 | $46,000 | $7,200 | 104 | $125 | $20,200 | $106,600 |

3TCO = ($36,000) + (80 × $125) + (((\$7,200) + (104 × $125)) × 3) = $106,600

In this example, we assumed it takes two hours per week to operate the systems (104 hours per year equals $20,200) and a 20 percent annual software maintenance fee ($7,200).

Here's another example: you want to implement a Crisis Communication Plan to help executive management retain control of your organization when the normal lines of communication are unavailable, such as during a massive cyberattack like NotPetya.

| AQC. COST | IMPL. HOURS | LABOR RATE | TOTAL IMPL. | ANNUAL RENEW $ | OPER- ATING HRS/YR | LABOR RATE | OPERAT- ING $/YR | 3TCO |
|---|---|---|---|---|---|---|---|---|
| $0 | 160 | $125 | $20,000 | $0 | 40 | $125 | $5,000 | $35,000 |

3TCO = ($0) + (160 × $125) + (((\$0) + (40 × $125)) × 3) = $35,000

In this example, we assumed there is a one-time cost to implement ($20,000) and there is one annual practice session ($5,000 each).

Run these same calculations for your own mitigations to figure out your own 3TCO.

Now you have a prioritized list of cyber risks to address, and you know the 3TCO for each one. Believe it or not, we haven't even gotten started yet! Here comes the real work: getting people to support all of your great ideas.

### PHASE 2, STEP 2: BUSINESS VALUE ANALYSIS

Your mitigations can create value for your company in four dimensions:

- Financial returns
- Technical risk mitigation
- Legal risk mitigation
- Increased reliability of operations

## Business Value Model

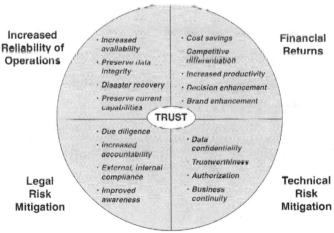

The purpose of doing a business value analysis is to take what could otherwise be an obscure set of decisions you're making related to cybersecurity and allow you to communicate the benefits of those actions to key decision makers (and later to everyone else) in business-friendly terms.

How do you do a business value analysis?

Let's take a closer look at the password manager we asked customer service to adopt earlier. The director of customer service doesn't necessarily know a lot about technology, cyber risks, or password protection. Their job is to serve customers. If you go to that director and say, "We are rolling out a new cybersecurity process for your department, which will require a new software," their reaction will likely be something like, "Why are you making my people do this? They're already busy enough. How is this plan of yours going to help us serve our customers better? I don't see the value in that." In short, they will protect their team from ever more disruptive changes. To be persuasive in that situation, you have to use language that makes sense to them. Use the business value analysis model to explain how your proposed changes will make their entire department better.

> If you can't explain the purpose behind your cyberse-
> curity changes in a way that gets buy-in from everyone,
> then your changes will fail.
>
> A great, quick primer for leading change in your organi-
> zation is the book *Buy-In: Saving Your Good Idea from
> Getting Shot Down* by John P. Kotter.
>
> You can quickly find this book on Amazon by following
> this link: http://b.link/buy-in.

Another way the business value model can be useful is when you have to justify spending money on cyberse-curity measures. For example, if a password manager for the entire customer service department represents a $25,000 annual expense, that money has to come from somewhere. You will be competing with other proposals for how your company should spend that $25,000. Some-one from the marketing department might propose to use that $25,000 to run a marketing campaign that would increase your top-line revenue by 2 percent. Someone from sales might say that they could hire three interns for the summer with that money and increase their number of outbound calls by 5 percent. When you're competing with all of those proposals, you need simple, straightfor-ward examples of how your cybersecurity measures will bring value to your business.

Now, let's get specific and do a business value analysis for these two risk mitigations:

- **Implement a crisis communication plan.** This will help executive management retain control of your organization when the normal lines of communication are unavailable, such as during a massive cyberattack like NotPetya.
- **Implement a next-generation malware control system.** Cyberattackers get more lethal with every new piece of malicious code they create, which requires us to regularly upgrade our defenses.

The major business benefit of the Crisis Communication Plan is *technical risk mitigation*. Why? Go back and look at the business value model and mark all the value factors that you think apply. Here's what I came up with:

- **Data confidentiality.** The Crisis Communication Plan reduces the risk of unauthorized disclosure, avoids the costs of breach notification, and reduces the risk of regulatory action.
- **Trustworthiness.** It increases confidence in the overall security of systems and processes.
- **Business continuity.** It increases our ability to recover and continue critical business functions and customer processes after a disaster.

There are some other benefits to a Crisis Communication Plan—such as decision enhancement (financial returns)—but no other single category lines up as well as *technical risk mitigation.* Use these three items, as well as any others, to help you make your case.

Now let's look at the second risk mitigation: implement a next-generation malware control system. At first glance, the mitigation might seem like an obvious technical risk mitigation. After all, a malware control system is a piece of technology. But not so fast! Go back and look at the business value model and mark all the value factors that you think apply. Here's what I came up with:

- **Increased availability.** It increases the availability of our technology to users in terms of actual outages and in terms of impaired response time, processing failures, noncompliance with service-level agreements, and so forth.
- **Preserve data integrity.** It maintains confidence in our data by helping to ensure accuracy or reducing the risk of data corruption.
- **Preserve current capabilities.** It maintains our current business capabilities so we don't fall behind serving customers as the cyberattackers become more virulent.

There are other benefits—such as data confidentiality (technical risk mitigation)—to implementing a next-generation malware control system. But again, no other single category lines up as well as *increased reliability of operations.* Use these three items, as well as any others, to help you make your case.

## PHASE 2, STEP 3: DASHBOARD AND ROAD MAP

Now that you've done multiple forms of analysis on your proposed mitigations, let's pull all of your cyber risk mitigations together into a simple dashboard and road map.

The dashboard is little more than a prioritized list of what you need to do. It's ordered by the size of the gap each mitigation will close and includes the 3TCO along with the primary and (optional) secondary business benefit. Here's an example that's based on sample data that's different than what I've already shown you.

| PRIORITY | MITIGATION NAME | BUSINESS VALUE | ESTIMATED IMPLE-MENTATION COST | ESTIMATED MAIN-TENANCE COSTS | 3TCO |
|---|---|---|---|---|---|
| 1 | Implement cyber-security training company-wide | Risk, Legal | $30,440 | $38,440 | $145,760 |
| 2 | Activate auto-en-crypt of USB storage company-wide | Risk, Reliability | $2,500 | $0 | $2,500 |
| 3 | Revise security requirements in contracts | Legal, Risk | $6,400 | $0 | $6,400 |
| 4 | Implement pass-word manager company-wide | Risk, Reliability | $27,940 | $38,440 | $143,260 |
| 5 | Improve governance of cybersecurity | Legal, Risk | $51,800 | $49,700 | $101,500 |
| 6 | Implement vulner-ability scanning | Risk, Reliability | $10,000 | $18,000 | $64,000 |
| 7 | Implement two-fac-tor authentication company-wide | Risk, Legal | $5,000 | $0 | $5,000 |

To increase your execution effectiveness, you might want to create an implementation road map, along with the dashboard. I'm not going to dive deeply into this topic because I've noticed a lot of variability across our customers when it comes to creating road maps. Some people like traditional Gantt charts while others want to use more LEAN/Agile tools and methods. If you're not sure what to use, check with your project management team if you have one. No obvious choice? Do a Google search for "Gantt chart Excel," and you'll see lots of tutorials to get you started.

As you develop your implementation road map, you may be tempted to change the order of the mitigations. If you do, make sure it's for a reasonable and defensible justification (write it down so you won't forget). It's possible, however unlikely, that you may be asked to explain your work in front of your biggest customer, an investor, a state regulator, or a judge and jury. A good justification would be to moderate the rate of change that your staff have to absorb. In the table above, notice that mitigations #3 (contracts), #5 (governance), and #6 (scanning) have little to no impact on staff. You might want to adjust their implementation sequence if you find that your people need a break from all the new cybersecurity practices you're putting in front of them.

## PHASE 2, STEP 4: INTERNAL MARKETING

Once you've recognized which gaps need to be plugged in your organization and you've decided what role everyone will play in your cyber risk management game plan, you have to continue to get buy-in. This is where the internal marketing becomes incredibly important. Ask yourself the following questions and communicate the answers to your company using several different communication channels, preferably well-established ones such as a newsletter and weekly team meetings. It's a great idea to partner with your marketing team as they will have useful tools and methods:

- What are our goals and objectives for implementing the next mitigation?
- How will we measure success?
- What is our time line for implementing these changes?
- Who will lead these changes?
- Do we need new hardware or software in order to enact our game plan?
- Will we need training for staff?
- How much will this mitigation cost, both in money and time?

## CYBERHYGIENE EXAMPLE

If your customer service department needs to use a password manager, it will not only provide technical risk mitigation, but it will also improve their productivity. You're actually making their lives easier because they no longer have to manually remember and enter a large number of usernames and passwords. (According to a 2017 report by LastPass, the average business employee must keep track of 191 passwords.)

Now when you approach your customer service department, who already think they're being overburdened by security procedures, you can say, "Look, based on the cyber risk scores we've collected and the business analysis we've conducted, we've found a potential problem with our password hygiene. We'd like your team to utilize a password manager throughout the department, which will actually make your lives easier and more productive." Once you explain to people how these cybersecurity measures will help them, it's likely they will buy in to your proposed changes. But you can only truly understand the business value of each change if you do a business value analysis.

## SMALL COMPANIES GET FTC SCRUTINY

Most of the examples in this book describe large, well-known brands. But don't let that fool you into thinking that small companies escape the scrutiny of the FTC.

In 2014, GMR Transcription Services was a small company with fewer than 50 employees that settled with the FTC. It was the FTC's fiftieth successful case.

GMR was charged with "inadequate data security measures which unfairly exposed the personal information of thousands of consumers on the open Internet, in some instances including consumers' medical histories and examination notes." Their charge resulted in a twenty-year FTC oversight of their information security program. What happened?

Medical transcription files prepared between March 2011 and October 2011 by Fedtrans, GMR's service provider, were indexed by a major Internet search engine and were publicly available to anyone using the search engine.

Some of the files contained notes from medical examinations of children and other highly sensitive medical data, such as information about psychiatric disorders, alcohol use, drug abuse, and pregnancy loss.

GMR's privacy statements and policies promised that "materials going through our system are highly secure and are never divulged to anyone." However, the company never required the individual typists it hired as contractors to implement security measures, such as installing antivirus software.

## PHASE 2, STEP 5: EXTERNAL MARKETING

If you are asked to explain your work in front of your biggest customer, an investor, a state regulator, or a judge and jury, you might want to take extra steps so your story is as clear as possible. Let me show you how to prepare a one-page scorecard that will put your entire cybersecurity story together.

## Summary Scorecard

| WHJ-597 | Actual | Target | Gap |
|---|---|---|---|
| IDENTIFY (ID) | 2.8 | 6.0 | 3.2 |
| PROTECT (PR) | 4.2 | 6.0 | 1.8 |
| DETECT (DE) | 2.6 | 6.0 | 3.4 |
| RESPOND (RS) | 3.5 | 6.0 | 2.5 |
| RECOVER (RC) | 4.3 | 6.0 | 1.8 |
| Overall Average | 3.5 | 6.0 | 2.5 |

## Top 5 Risks

| NIST Activities (sorted by Gap Size) | Actual | Target | Gap |
|---|---|---|---|
| 1. Detection Processes (DE.DP) | 1.4 | 6.0 | 4.6 |
| 2. Governance (ID.GV) | 1.8 | 6.0 | 4.2 |
| 3. Response Improvements (RS.IM) | 2.5 | 6.0 | 3.5 |
| 4. Recovery Comm. (RC.CO-1) | 2.5 | 6.0 | 3.5 |
| 5. Anomalies and Events (DE.AE) | 2.6 | 6.0 | 3.4 |

In this simple example, I've placed the two tables we created in phase 1 (chapter 5) across the top and then inserted the radar diagram across the bottom. You can mix and match this in whatever way will work best for your audience. Use our online Cyber Risk Workbook to automate the creation of your tables and the radar diagram. You can access it here: http://b.link/cyber-risk-workbook.

The easiest way I've found to create the scorecard is to paste the tables and the radar diagram onto a blank Microsoft PowerPoint slide. Here are a few other tips:

- Since the scorecard is meant to be seen by outsiders, *do not* put your company name or logo on it. Sounds crazy to say that, right? Typically, you would put your logo on everything you release to outsiders, but in this case, your scorecard probably contains information about temporary weaknesses you would not want to fall into the wrong hands.
- On that note, you should strictly limit who has access to all the data you gathered, analyzed, and used to create this scorecard. Follow a need-to-know approach for sharing the data.
- If you can, obtain a signed nondisclosure agreement (NDA) before you show them the scorecard. This provides another layer of protection.
- Also, put a label at the bottom indicating the confidentiality of this data. If you have no guidelines for

labeling, you could use this: "Company Restricted—Do Not Distribute without Signed NDA."

· Because you will create future versions of the scorecard that reflect your progress, be sure to put the published date in the footer.

· Finally, notice in the example that the code WHJ-597 appears in the upper-left and bottom-right corners. When we work with customers, we assign a random "license plate" to their cyber risk records instead of using their names. That way, if we lost control of that data (total nightmare!), the data is already anonymized to protect them.

## THE CHOICE TO MOVE FORWARD

You've identified and prioritized your company's top cyber risks, and you've developed a plan to manage those risks, including how to get buy-in from decision makers and your employees, and how to determine your budgeting needs. Without making these changes, you put your company and your customers in danger of losing valuable information, resources, their reputation, and potentially causing physical harm.

Companies like AsusTek (remember them from the start of part 2?) make mistakes all the time, and almost none of them communicate their cybersecurity failures publicly. With the plan you've developed in phase 2, you can not only reduce the risk of a large number of cybersecurity breaches, but when you do experience a breach, you can also use it as an opportunity to build trust with your customers.

You could implement every facet of your plan to perfection—and do everything you learned in phases 1 and 2—and your work still wouldn't be done. Now that you've improved your organization's cyberhygiene, you must continue executing and maintaining your cyber risk management game plan.

Remember, cybersecurity isn't what you buy; it's what you *do*.

# PHASE 3

## MAINTENANCE AND UPDATES

In early 2017, unknown cyberattackers broke into the Equifax network. They were able to do so because Equifax practiced terrible cyberhygiene. We don't know who perpetrated the attack, but we do know that based on the extent of the breach, they were a very sophisticated team of experts.

After they infiltrated Equifax, they then mapped out the entire network where credit information was stored. After they identified everything of value, they consolidated multiple gigabytes of information, which they then transferred out of the Equifax network—*undetected*. In short, they stole the credit files of every working American.

There is nothing about this attack that would suggest

it was the work of an opportunist or a political activist. Everything we know suggests it was deliberately calculated to be silent and designed to inflict the maximum amount of theft. We don't know yet what the long-term consequences are of that theft. That is not a good sign.

The lack of a clear indication for how the thief will use all this data suggests that the motivation for stealing the data was not personal gain. The motivation for stealing it was bigger and possibly more insidious. My guess is that it's being stockpiled for future use. If a foreign government wanted to weaken the United States, as they did when interfering with our last presidential election, they could use this information to compromise our entire credit-granting system.

Imagine what our economy would be like if a significant number of credit files were altered or riddled with fraudulent entries. Normal people who want to buy a house or a car would be unable to do so. Even though the derogatory marks in our credit files wouldn't be legitimate, it would throw sand in the gears of our economy and seriously dampen our economic growth.

This attack has massive implications. If you go back and look at how Equifax attempted to respond with their public announcement of the data breach, they made a large number of missteps. Some of the mistakes they made were tragic: in one instance on Twitter, while trying to direct people to their site to see if they were affected, Equifax accidentally sent followers to a phishing site.

Of course, bigger than the mistakes they made in their response was the mistake they made by not patching their Internet-facing web servers. Their cyberhygiene was so bad that the attackers didn't even have to phish them. They were able to break in quickly and roam the Equifax network for one hundred days undetected.

Equifax was trusted to protect massive amounts of sensitive data, and they blew it. That data breach hurt our entire community, not just a single company or a single person. Although your company may not handle as much sensitive data as Equifax, you still have an obligation to yourself, your customers, and our community to protect the digital assets you do have to the best of your abilities.

You won't be able to protect those assets with a one-time implementation of your cyber risk management game plan. You must maintain it and update it over time. You need to be better than Equifax. And you will be.

## DYNAMIC, NOT STATIC

One of the most important elements of maintaining your cyber risk management game plan is doing check-ins and reviews with your team, not only to gauge your progress toward reasonable cybersecurity but also to celebrate wins and update your scorecard. The scores that you acquired in phase 1 are not static. Those scores for each item on the questionnaire can and should change over time.

> Phases 1 and 2 each lasted a month, and phase 3 takes place over the following ten months to make a full year.

## CONTINUALLY UPDATE YOUR SCORECARDS

It's one thing to implement change, but it's another thing entirely to document and track it. Therefore, you want to track your successes and generate new scorecards every ninety days. If you end up having a difficult conversation with a regulator or a customer, having up-to-date cybersecurity scorecards could become invaluable evidence that you are practicing reasonable cybersecurity.

Updating your scores creates a story. You can tell a regulator, "A year ago, when we did our first cyber risk assessment, we averaged a 3.6 in detecting cybersecurity incidents. However, after five quarters of sustained effort, we have improved our score to a 5.1." You will then be able to articulate to them exactly what measures you've taken to improve your score. Rather than speaking in unsubstantiated generalities—as most executives do when they talk about cybersecurity—you can give people a data-driven narrative to *prove* that you're practicing reasonable cybersecurity.

## SCHEDULE MONTHLY CHECK-INS

Aside from taking the time to update your cyber risk scores, it is also important to preschedule a full year of monthly cybersecurity check-ins. These check-ins take about an hour and should recur on the same day and time each month, which establishes consistency.

When you schedule these meetings, be selective about who is in attendance. Focus on the handful of people who will make the most difference to your success. These do not need to be large meetings. They should be tactical meetings instead. The point is to monitor progress and to know when progress is impeded so that you can remove the impediment. Too many people will bog down that process, so keep it small.

You already know what you're actively working on for cybersecurity. These meetings are simply an opportunity to update each other on what parts of your plan you're currently executing and what you plan on doing before the next monthly meeting. It's also an opportunity to look at your cyber risk management game plan to make sure you are on track with your objectives.

If you are offtrack, your solution might be a simple one. It may be that there is no one available with the skillset you need to mitigate a particular cyber risk. In that scenario, that's a human resources problem, which is easy enough to tackle: you will hire someone, or contract with someone, to help you solve the problem.

Similarly, another impediment that could arise is if you have a major corporate change underway, which consumes all of the energy in your company. People have a hard enough time handling one change at a time, let alone multiple changes. If you're experiencing larger changes in your company, you may need to hit the Pause button on certain aspects of your game plan.

Holding these monthly meetings also allows new information to come to light, which will alter your cyber risk management game plan. As rigorous as your data gathering will be, you could still discover something in the execution of the plan that you didn't already know. For example, you may realize that your Protect function is weaker than you thought. In situations like this, take it as an opportunity to reconnect with your original purpose. What was it that caused you to begin this journey in the first place? Why do you even want reasonable cybersecurity? What's really at stake? If you can reconnect with that purpose, it's easier to act when unexpected information comes your way.

## CELEBRATE YOUR WINS

These meetings can also be a time to celebrate things that your organization is doing well. How exactly you go about celebrating is purely a cultural choice, but it's more important than you might realize. Yes, people should get recognition when they do anything well, but if you celebrate cybersecurity wins in a way that's different from your other company celebrations, then it reinforces the counterproductive narrative that cyber risks are separate from other business matters. If you celebrate reaching a cybersecurity milestone and you celebrate it like any other business win, then people will start to recognize it as part of their regular business life.

## COMMON CYBERSECURITY
## COMMUNICATION FAILURES

The same concept applies for all communication about your cyber risk management game plan. A big mistake I see executives make is sending out an email with a request and assume that they've communicated with everyone, which is almost never true. What happens instead is that some small percentage of people will read the email, and the people who don't read it are the ones who are so busy that they *need* the information in the email.

That doesn't mean you shouldn't send emails. It just means that you need a multichannel communication strategy. This strategy should involve sending the same messages in multiple ways so that you can reach as many people as possible, because different people are watching different channels. Just because someone gets an email doesn't mean they're going to read it. But if that information also shows up in a company newsletter and is passed on in the weekly management meeting, it will reach more people.

Moreover, department meetings are great opportunities to add cybersecurity updates to the agenda. That update could be in the form of text that's given to the department head running the meeting, or it could be a guest appearance from you, the executive sponsor of the cybersecurity initiative. You could use this opportunity to let people know what plan you and the rest of the company are executing going forward with cybersecurity.

## IDENTIFY NEXT STEPS

The final item on your monthly meeting agenda is to discuss what comes next. If your actual scores match your target score in one cybersecurity function, you can close out that project and move down your prioritized list to the next project.

If your physical security is lacking because people don't have access control badges with their photograph on it, your project might be to start implementing photographs on the badges. You create the project, purchase the systems necessary to get everyone badged and photographed, and create an administrative process so that every new member of the organization will also get a badge. Your project has now created the *ongoing* capability of badging people with photographs. As soon as you have handed that off to your physical security team and they are operating it, you have mitigated the risk, that particular project is finished, and it's time to update your cyber risk records and change priorities.

## SCHEDULE QUARTERLY REVIEWS

Whereas your monthly meetings are tactical in nature, the purpose of the quarterly review is to take a step back and look at where you are overall every ninety days. The assumption is that over the previous ninety days, you've implemented a number of risk mitigations and have increased many of your scores.

This is your opportunity to set and manage expectations about product progress, risk reduction, and the business value you're creating. Make sure to remind people that not only have you reduced risks, but you've actually delivered on the other business value you've identified, such as increasing people's productivity. Highlighting the business value you're delivering to the organization is key in these quarterly meetings.

## TAKE IN THE BROADER PICTURE

Another item on your quarterly agenda should be looking across the cybersecurity landscape outside your organization.

Before 2012, one of the most important handwashing techniques to prevent malware was to make sure that every computer had the most recent signatures or fingerprints for every different type of malicious code currently floating around the Internet. Most antivirus packages have hundreds of thousands, or even millions, of malware signatures, one for each unique digital cootie they've encountered. The theory was that once the antivirus companies saw that new piece of malicious code on your computer, they could instantly recognize it and make sure it didn't cause any trouble.

Therefore, having malware signatures distributed as quickly as possible by your antivirus system to your fleet of computers, multiple times per day if possible, was a very big deal. People became good at doing that. But when cybercriminals realized they were no longer able to easily perpetrate this kind of attack, they figured out a great countermeasure. If they could release the malicious code in a way so that every instance of the code had a different signature, our whole defense would fall apart. That's exactly what they did. The end of the era of signature-based defenses was documented in the *MIT Technology Review* in June 2012. Today, if your major defense against malicious code is relying only on updating signatures as fast as possible, you're more exposed than you realize.

That's why you have to keep an eye out for the changing world of cybersecurity around you. You may have to purchase completely different products, train your staff on completely new things, or you may have to update your processes based on changes to the cybersecurity landscape beyond your company.

## INVITE MORE PEOPLE

Quarterly meetings will differ from your monthly meetings in that more people should be in attendance. Monthly meetings are very focused on accomplishments and achieving particular goals in the implementation of risk mitigations. The quarterly meeting is more focused on keeping people informed about what is going on and steering the overall cyber risk management game plan. If you sell products in a highly regulated industry—such as banking, insurance, or health care—your sales people may regularly encounter questions about your cybersecurity because these types of companies are required by laws and regulations to perform due diligence on their suppliers and vendors. This meeting is a good way to help the sales leaders keep track of important issues that could be an impediment to them closing deals.

## FIELD QUESTIONS AND PRACTICE INTERNAL REPUTATION MANAGEMENT

Any questions proposed by the stakeholders should be given close consideration. Your ability to practice reasonable cybersecurity will be dependent on the favor shown by the most important stakeholders, so use this meeting as an opportunity to practice reputation management for your cyber risk management game plan. If the game plan has fallen out of favor in your company, this quarterly meeting is a chance to take the temperature of the room and gauge what exactly is making people anxious so you can take action.

## ADJUST YOUR SCORES

The most important aspect of the quarterly meeting is to change the scores on your original cyber risk scorecard.

You don't conduct interviews again; you simply need to update your spreadsheet with all of the new scores based on your actual progress.

As your company completes risk mitigations, you can track how the scores have improved over time. If the cybersecurity landscape outside of your company has changed and risk is going up as a result, even your best efforts may not reduce your risks. Identify new and evolving risks—both inside and outside of your company—and discuss whether or not you think these threats are serious enough to officially change your scores and subsequently alter your overall priorities.

## SCHEDULE AN ANNUAL CYBERSECURITY SUMMIT

Your annual cybersecurity summit will cover much of the same territory as your monthly and quarterly meetings. The major difference will be that your summit will have a broader scope. In short, your summit will summarize your annual progress and set you up to repeat phases 1, 2, and 3 over the next twelve months.

### OLD VERSUS NEW SCORECARDS

Be sure to display your old scorecard and compare it to your newest scores, highlighting the changes your company has made to improve your cybersecurity.

This is a time to celebrate the great accomplishments you've made and encourage the various stakeholders who have made this all possible. Let them know that you are all going into a new year and will have a new set of top cyber risks. Together, you will manage those new risks once again.

Reenergize the company. You've washed, you've rinsed, and you're about to repeat.

## STRUCTURED, SYSTEMATIC, AND COMPREHENSIVE

During the annual cybersecurity summit, prepare people for the fact that you will be doing a new round of interviews in the new year.

Why?

As Peter Drucker, one of the best-known and most widely influential thinkers and writers on the subject of management theory and practice, said in his book *The Effective Executive*:

"After asking what needs to be done, the effective executive sets priorities and sticks to them...After completing the original top-priority task(s), the executive resets priorities. He asks, 'What must be done now?' This generally results in new and different priorities.

The annual interviews are your way of asking, 'What must be done now to practice reasonable cybersecurity?'"

The process of practicing reasonable cyber hygiene is systematic, comprehensive, and highly structured. Once you finish the annual summit and reach the natural end to phase 3, you will go back to the beginning and start over with data gathering.

Not only will this process help manage cyber risks and add business value to your company, but it will also help you tell a complete story if your company experiences a data breach. This story is what you will tell important stakeholders, judges, and even outside regulators and proves you are not negligent. That story will be bolstered by comprehensive interviews, a series of minutes from your monthly meetings, detailed scorecards, and much more. All these artifacts can save the day for you and your company in the case of a cybersecurity failure so you won't face the same fate as Equifax and their customers, even on a smaller scale.

## WHAT IS YOUR STORY?

As you progress on your cybersecurity journey, you will continuously build and tell a story to the people around you. How you tell that story greatly affects how supportive and committed everyone in your organization is to cyber-security. This third phase of your cyber risk management plan is an opportunity for you to share that story with your stakeholders.

You're asking people to change how they operate on a daily basis. You need a story that they can understand.

Use these monthly, quarterly, and annual meetings to tell the story of your shared journey.

# CONCLUSION

## CYBERSECURITY IS THE QUALITY OF THE JOURNEY, NOT A DESTINATION

Fire has posed the same risks to us since the beginning of time. It's not innovating anytime soon. You can follow the well-established fire-prevention checklists, conduct an annual fire drill in your building, and buy a blanket fire insurance policy that protects you and your company and forget about it. Cybersecurity risks, however, are constantly evolving, and so are the criminals who create those risks. If you want to survive in the cyberrich world of the future, you must evolve along with them.

That might seem like too tall of an order for you. You're no cybersecurity expert. The threats facing your company's digital assets may seem nebulous and threatening, but there is a framework you can employ to manage those risks. By following the NIST Cybersecurity Framework and the three-phase cyber risk management game plan you created in this book, you can stay one step ahead of your competition.

There is no such thing as perfect cybersecurity prevention, at home or while you travel for work. But by using the handwashing techniques and tools I've given you in this book, you can greatly reduce your risk on a continuous basis. Because cybersecurity is not a destination. Reasonable cybersecurity is a function of the quality of *the journey*.

Based on the concepts and tools in part 1 of this book, your next step in the journey is to create your game plan, as outlined in part 2. Remember that you cannot do this alone. Share this book with other executives and leaders in your company and ask them to cosponsor the implementation of your game plan. You're not weak or stupid if you ask for help; you're simply acknowledging that you're learning something new and that reasonable cybersecurity is a team sport.

Having said that, you are now equipped with everything you need to start and continue a high-quality cybersecurity journey on your own, but it's always easier to navigate through unknown territory with a guide.

Cyber Risk Opportunities would be pleased to be that guide for you. You can contact us by emailing info@cyberriskopportunities.com or by visiting http://b.link/program. On that page, you'll find a summary of our full-featured services, including a link to the Cyber Risk Workbook that automates everything you learned in the lite version detailed in this book.

Good luck on your journey, and remember, fire doesn't innovate, but cyber risks do.

# APPENDIX

## CYBERSECURITY CHECKLIST
## FOR EXECUTIVES

1. Nobody can reliably detect *all* phishing attempts; however, you can test your skills here: opendns.com/phishing-quiz.
2. Do not open email attachments or click links on emails you didn't expect to receive.
3. Never automatically say yes to unexpected prompts to install or update software.
4. Use a nonadmin account for daily tasks such as emailing and web browsing.
5. Turn on Windows Defender.
6. Back up your data locally *and* in the cloud.
7. Avoid public Wi-Fi.

8. Use an ad blocker on your computer and mobile phone.
9. On your phone, only download apps directly from Apple and Google.
10. On your computer, only download software from reputable sites.
11. Turn on automatic updates.
12. Never pay a ransom to get back control of your data or systems.
13. Look at your credit score at least once per quarter to detect large drops.
14. Freeze your credit files at each major bureau.
15. Set up alerts on all major accounts to detect suspicious activity.
16. Protect your mobile phone number with a PIN.
17. Use a high-quality password manager such as 1Password or LastPass.
18. Set nonobvious answers to security questions and store them in your password manager.
19. Turn on two-factor authentication on every account that allows it.
20. Verify all electronic funds transfer instructions before acting on them.
21. Turn on encryption for all data backups.
22. Take a burner laptop and phone for work travel.
23. Utilize a virtual private network (VPN), especially while traveling.

24. Upon return from work travel, reset all devices to factory settings.
25. Do not widely advertise your travel plans on social media.
26. Let your bank, credit card company, financial advisor, and so forth know when you'll be traveling.
27. Establish a cyber risk management game plan for your company.

# ACKNOWLEDGMENTS

Once the manuscript for this book was finished, I reflected on how I got to this point in my professional life. I knew I had help, but until I started making a list, I didn't realize how many people directly supported and encouraged me along the way.

Wow!

I'm blessed.

I deeply love and appreciate my wife, Nally, who provides me and our family with support beyond our expectations.

And I'm grateful to our children, Alex, Madison, Tiyos, Ava, Ruby, and Rose, for inspiring me to be the best dad possible in the face of never-ending work demands. I love each one of you very much.

Thanks to my longtime friends Marc Menninger, Larry Roberts, Mike Pavlu, Steve Madden, and Mike Evans for being there whenever I need help.

This book, and my entrepreneurial journey, wouldn't exist without my present and past teammates at Cyber Risk Opportunities: Daryl Harper, Rob Finch, Brennan Harper, Pat Fahey, Nisha Kaippilly, Jamie Brown, Nancy Avera, Justin Pierce, and Cynthia Cerda.

So much of the content in this book is the result of the requests, feedback, and support of our customers and partners. In particular, thank you Glenn Joiner, Jeff Jones, Ralph Johnson, John-Luke Peck, Jake Bernstein, Lee Marsh, Drew Dorben, Raquel Liberman, Bill Baumann, Jon Hocut, Chris Anderson, Carmen Marsh, Michael Cockrill, Evan Smith, and Phil Conrod.

Operating a business requires a wide range of specialized skills, most of which I either don't have or do not have enough of to be successful. In those areas, I have benefited from the following amazing mentors and coaches: Dan Stull, Greg Larson, Jay Soroka, Jared Pfost, Marc Goodman, Raj Samani, Steve Nelson, and Adam Shostack.

My first formal chief information security officer (CISO) role was at PEMCO Insurance in Seattle, Washington. I want to thank Jack Brown for hiring me, Steve Ricco for challenging me to describe the business value of cyber-security, and Josh Schmidt for helping me *figure out* the business value of cybersecurity. Thanks also to Kimberly Prentiss, Ken Swanson, Jenee Byrd, Stuart Sabel, Dick Shay, Hal Garyn, Mark Yeoell, and Joel Scambray.

The one place where I learned the most (and the best) lessons about world-class information security was at Stanford Research Institute (SRI) International. Thank you, Doug Webb, Donn Parker, Doug Dickson, Ric Steinberger, Rick Millar, John Vajda, Gene Schultz, Karen Worstell, Jim Maloney, Steve Whitlock, Jim Reavis, and Josh Leewarner.

While at SRI, I worked with some amazing customers and partners. My standout experiences were with Vick Perry at his startup, Vitessa, and the FedLine for Windows team: Tom Gagnon, Gordon Tannura, and Michael H. Lloyd Davies.

The one place where I learned the most (and the best) lessons about leadership was at Expeditors International. Thank you, Chris McClincy, Roland Faragher-Horwell, Nate Lynch, Megan Knight, Lisa Benze, kp Ramsdale, Ted Koslowsky, Mike Pederson, and John O'Neill.

Thank you, Dr. Marilyn Gist, for delivering the most transformative experiences I ever had in the classroom.

It happened during the 2007–2008 Executive Leadership program cohort at Seattle University. I've drawn on those experiences almost every day since then.

Finally, I want to acknowledge and thank the United States Air Force for getting me started in what was then called computer security. In particular, I want to give a shout out to the fantastic people of the 83rd Fighter Weapons Squadron at Tyndall AFB, Florida, and the F-22 Systems Program Office at Wright-Patterson AFB, Ohio.

# ABOUT THE AUTHOR

**KIP BOYLE** is the founder and CEO of Cyber Risk Opportunities, whose mission is to help executives thrive as cyber risk managers. His customers have included the US Federal Reserve Bank, Boeing, Visa, Intuit, Mitsubishi, DuPont, and many others. A cybersecurity expert since 1992, he was previously the director of wide area network security for the Air Force's F-22 Raptor program and a senior consultant for Stanford Research Institute (SRI). Kip has a graduate certificate in executive leadership and a master's in business management. He lives in the Seattle area with his wife and six children.